PRACTICE EDUCATION

in

SOCIAL WORK

3rd edition

Achieving Professional Standards

PRACTICE EDUCATION in SOCIAL WORK

3rd edition

Achieving Professional Standards

PAULA BEESLEY AND SUE TAPLIN

Authors of the first and second editions:
Pam Field, Cathie Jasper, Lesley Littler and Liz Munro

CRITICAL SKILLS FOR SOCIAL WORK

Routledge
Taylor & Francis Group

LONDON AND NEW YORK

First edition published in 2013 by Critical Publishing Ltd

Second edition published in 2016
This third edition published in 2023

Published 2025 by Routledge
4 Park Square, Milton Park, Abingdon, Oxon OX14 4RN
605 Third Avenue, New York, NY 10017

Routledge is an imprint of the Taylor & Francis Group, an informa business

British Library Cataloguing in Publication Data
A CIP record for this book is available from the British Library

ISBN: 9781041056546 (hbk)
ISBN: 9781915713094 (pbk)
ISBN: 9781041056553 (ebk)

The rights of Paula Beesley and Sue Taplin to be identified as the Authors of this work has been asserted by them in accordance with the Copyright, Design and Patents Act 1988.

We would also like to acknowledge and extend our thanks to Pam Field, Cathie Jasper, Lesley Littler and Liz Munro who were the authors of the first and second editions of this book.

Cover design by Out of House Ltd
Text design by Greensplash

DOI: 10.4324/9781041056553

Contents

Meet the **authors**

Paula Beesley is a registered social worker with a background in working within children services, particularly with parents with a learning disability. She is a qualified practice educator and has supported numerous students, both in her role in local authority teams and as an independent off-site practice educator (OSPE). She now works at Leeds Beckett University as a senior lecturer in social work, specialising in skill development and placement preparation and support. She has written her doctoral thesis on developing knowledge and skills in social work student supervision.

Sue Taplin is a registered social worker with 18 years' experience as a social work researcher and university lecturer. Prior to embarking on an academic career, Sue practised in the voluntary sector as a palliative care social worker and practice educator. Sue currently works at the University of Gloucestershire, where she brings her passion for practice and interprofessional learning and teaching to the undergraduate and postgraduate social work programmes. Sue is the editor of *Innovations in Practice Learning*, published by Critical Publishing in 2018.

Foreword

I am writing this Foreword as I celebrate a half-century since my own social work education. As a postgraduate, I was able to undertake a one-year training to gain an award called the Certificate of Qualification in Social Work (CQSW), and in that single year I experienced no less than three placements. Each of these I remember as though it were yesterday. The first was two days a week at the Grimsby office of the Probation Service. I was the first student that my practice educator (or student supervisor as we called them) had taken on placement and it was here that I was able to kindle a growing love of groupwork. My second placement was residential – four weeks in the adolescent unit of a psychiatric hospital, where I sometimes did nights. It was very challenging in its intensity, and it was my first encounter with interprofessional team-work. The third and final placement was full time at Hull Social Services Department in the team that worked on the Bransholme estate, said to be the largest council housing estate in Europe. My supervisor was on the cusp of retirement and left me to sink or swim, in contrast to my Grimsby experience where I had been keenly nurtured. I benefited from both approaches in their very different ways.

Much has changed in 50 years. The context for my own practice learning was the community. Large social services departments had just been established, amalgamating all the specialist social work services into a unitary one in which generic social workers worked with people *from cradle to grave*. My student supervisors were experienced practitioners but they had very little, if any, training as teachers of practice. My practice learning was assessed as Pass or Fail in a brief report written by my supervisors, a report to which neither my clients (as we then called service users) nor I contributed.

I was exposed to groupwork from my very first placement, and probation work was still in the social work family, with about a third of my fellow students going on to practise in that field. There was much debate over the respective value of block and concurrent placements – whether we were in placement part time or full time, with my own training encompassing both types, plus the residential. The technology of placements relied on typewriters for recording (we had just one in the Hull Social Services team office and you had to wait your turn) and buses for transport – they were cheap, frequent and reliable.

Though much has changed, much is also the same. In particular, the value that students take from their learning in practice, as demonstrated by the way placements stay in our memories. Let us explore some of the other themes that were a feature of practice education then and that have remained consistently so.

The private nature of supervision sessions

Some years after my own education as a social worker, and following the 15 years that I supervised students on placement with me, I became an external examiner for practice education programmes. What this meant in practice was the sampling of work by the candidates, the practice educators in training. A couple of these programmes required the candidates to video record one or two supervision sessions – ie the time they spent one-to-one to facilitate the student's practice learning, usually once a week for about an hour and a half. This was a rare and privileged glimpse into an event that few others witness; apart from group supervision, which is rare, social work supervision is experienced only by the dyad of supervisor and student. This dyad writes about supervision, reflects on it and gathers evidence from it, but all of this is indirect as far as non-participants are concerned. What goes on in supervision, and how it goes on, remains intensely private and relatively unresearched (with some notable exceptions), just as it was 50 years ago, yet it is considered to be the lynchpin of the practice education relationship, and the core for reflective learning. We need to map what actually takes place in supervision and replace speculation with observation, in order to know better what works and what works well.

It is anecdotal evidence, but I drew two lessons from my own observations of the videoed supervision sessions that I witnessed: first, the most successful ones were those where the balance of talk was roughly even, and if not quite even, then slightly in favour of student over educator; and second, those practice educators who introduced activity into the session seemed to provoke better participative learning. I am thinking of a practice educator who used a sand-tray in the session and another who introduced a board game, tailored to the student's learning needs. Introducing an activity, often facilitated through an object of some sort, is evidence of other attributes, too: forward planning, imagination, thinking outside of the session about the student's specific learning needs, and stepping outside comfort zones. All of this seems to contribute to student learning. The least successful sessions were the cosy *'how's it going?'* ones, where neither party was willing or able to take a risk.

The private nature of practice, live teaching and the direct involvement of service users

As a student, much of my practice learning took place in the homes of the people I was working with. In parallel with the experience of the supervision session, this was almost always a private encounter, with my supervisor/practice educator relying on my reports of these engagements in a subsequent supervision session. When I became a practice educator, I was determined that the two of us, the student and me, would spend as much time as possible working and learning together, certainly in those first few formative weeks of the placement. Initially, the student would take a back seat in the practice but would be expected to take the lead in the subsequent sharing of observations and giving feedback; as the student's confidence and experience grew, they would take the lead in the practice encounters, and I would facilitate the subsequent observations and feedback. With an able student, I would often find myself experiencing true co-working quite soon, but the model was flexible enough to accommodate different degrees of confidence.

This way of learning/working had been instinctive and unformalised. However, when I later became involved in practice educator training, I became interested in the notion of live teaching as a more formal model of helping students learn with service users in the same room. This brought the supervision session into the service user's own home, involving them as direct participants in the teaching – as experts by experience and not 'just' users of services. The model was popular when I taught it in the workshop setting, but it became evident in the follow-up workshops that it had been far from easy to put into practice. That is no discredit to live teaching as a model – worthwhile things often require effort, even struggle – but it does suggest that a live teaching model needs more work and perhaps different ways of practising it.

Direct observations have become embedded in practice education in a way that was absent 50 years ago. However, direct observation goes only so far – like the driving test examiner who is required not to intervene. On the other hand, live teaching gives the practice educator (and the service user) a parallel set of controls by which the car can be driven: in other words, the facility to intervene there and then to help the student's immediate learning in practice. Even an emergency stop if required!

Integrating academy and agency, theory and practice

If live teaching is a means of integrating supervision-session learning with learning on-site, how could this same integration be achieved in terms of class-based learning and practice-based learning? My own experience 50 years ago was of 'two courses', academy and agency, seemingly different worlds apart. Has this changed much in the half-century? Certainly, there are models that attempt to close that gap, like apprenticeships – but perhaps the gap is something to be celebrated? One of the struggles for students in wholly agency-based learning is how to carve out a role as a student when they are still seen as a worker. In class, students might be exposed to role-played simulations and to presentations by practice educators and experts by experience as a way of bringing the field into the class. All of this is undoubtedly valuable, but it has a 'compensatory' feel to it.

A similar classic struggle is the integration of theory and practice. I have elsewhere likened many practitioners' perspectives on this as oil and vinegar: with vigorous shaking they will emulsify as one, but without continuous effort they soon part into their natural states of separation. I think this comes from seeing theory as somehow identified with the academy, and practice with the agency. There is talk of '*applying theory*' as though it were a dressing. Happily, we have developed more sophisticated – and yet, in some ways, simpler – notions of theory arising from practice. We – students, educators, service users – are theorising all the time. Certainly, we make hypotheses to explain what is happening. Making sense of this process and making it explicit in ourselves and in others is likely to be more valuable to practice development than exertions to squeeze it into a formal Theory with a capital 'T'. This process of starting with practice also enables us to move from the idea of evidence-based practice to that of practice-based evidence.

I mentioned that the structure of placement learning – block or concurrent – was contentious 50 years ago. That discussion is largely dormant now, but it is one that I would like to resurrect. Having been largely in favour of full-time placements, I have rebalanced my opinion. I think the opportunities for a greater integration of student learning by means of a week that is partly spent in class and partly in the field has much merit, depending on how that time is spent, of course. These thoughts have been crystallised by a recent sabbatical at a Chilean university where the students on the five-year BSW programme have concurrent placements through the last three years. The proportion of time spent on placement starts at one and a half days a week in Year 3 and grows with each year. The students are increasingly responsible for presenting and sharing their practice learning in student-led workshops during their classes in the university. Moreover, the first periods of practice learning are spent in the same community, working together with that community to identify needs and wants, followed by an action plan, and finally putting the plan into effect. Only after this year of community-based practice learning do students work with individual service users and families in Years 4 (two days a week) and 5 (three days a week).

Learning in non-traditional placements

The formal curriculum tells us something about a profession's current priorities and concerns – what it thinks it is about – but it is the settings for its placements that immediately reveal a profession's hand. Current priorities in the UK are for placements where students can experience statutory work (that is, work that is mandated and regulated by law) and with contrasting service user groups – usually one with children and one with adults. It is useful for today's students to learn that these priorities have changed over time, and to know that they will change again. As I have outlined earlier, the balance in my own placements was achieved according to the type of social work – groupwork, residential work, community-based practice.

Placements that break the contemporary orthodoxy of statutory and age-based divisions (children and adults) are referred to as non-traditional placements. There was a notable flowering of these after the introduction of the social work degree, with some of the most innovative ones developed in organisations led by service users. The availability of a daily placement fee enabled the payment for independent off-site supervision by qualified social workers, while day-to-day supervision was undertaken by service users in the organisation.

Another significant non-traditional placement is the international one. There were no opportunities for international placements 50 years ago (though Grimsby sometimes seemed like another land). In my cohort of 29 students, two were international students (Zimbabwe and Hong Kong) and the rest of the cohort was White, 16 women and 13 men, a gender ratio of 11:9. Placements abroad were a growing feature of social work practice learning, but the global pandemic and Brexit have clipped these wings. My experiences of Chilean social work recounted earlier demonstrate the significant learning that can come from exposure to different cultures and contexts, and we must do all we can to restore the opportunities afforded by international placements.

Contingency plans – the elephant in the room

Practice educators have a profound duty not just to help novice social workers develop their love for social work, but also to protect future service users and ensure they will be in safe hands. So, practice teaching cannot be separated from practice assessment. The placement is where an experienced social worker decides whether the student should continue their studies and, ultimately, be allowed into the social work profession.

Few students failed their practice learning 50 years ago, just as now. Whether this is a good thing or a bad thing, practice educators need to consider contingency plans for those relatively rare occasions when they have concerns about a student's ability or suitability for the profession. We recognise the ability to initiate and engage in difficult conversations as a significant skill for social workers, so it ought to be part of their repertoire when acting in the role of practice educator. It helps if the dyad has discussed this contingency from the very beginning of the placement: too often 'magical thinking' can encourage people to believe that talking about something will bring it on, while in fact the reverse is true. One practice educator keeps a stuffed toy elephant in view to remind him and others always to talk about any elephant in the room – taboo topics that will fester if they are not acknowledged.

Critical social work practice learning

It was 50 years ago that I first heard the phrase *'we want social workers who can hit the ground running'* and it's still up and running. It is understandable that hard-pressed managers want education programmes to turn out cogs that will fit their particular wheels and, of course, social workers must be competent to fulfil their duties. However, the best social workers are those who know how to adapt to rapidly changing circumstances – the *'moving carpet'* as it is described later in this book. They need to learn how to apply general values and principles to highly specific instances. To achieve this, social work education in general and practice education in particular must hone the student's capacity for critical thinking.

Social workers need to be competent to feed into the policy-making process, both at the local and the global level, and this requires a critical awareness. On a day-to-day basis, social workers' first loyalty is to their service users and a generalised notion of professional good practice. This has the potential to put them at odds with their employer, but the best employers know that assertive and purposively critical social workers who fight for best practices offer, in the long run, the best safeguard to the agency's reputation; and agencies that provide placements that nurture critical thinking will attract these same students as future employees.

I hope you have enjoyed this glimpse at the practice education album of 50 years ago, and the comparisons with today. Despite the obvious differences, what strikes me is how many of the fundamental themes endure and, no doubt, will do so for the coming years. Enjoy the journey ahead, as you explore these themes in further detail in the pages of this fascinating book.

Professor Mark Doel
Sheffield Hallam University

Chapter 1 | Introduction

Welcome and thank you for reading this book. This is a book for everyone involved in practice education in social work. It offers guidance on the key knowledge and skills that practice educators need in order to support and assess social work students, to enable their learning, and to manage their placements. It has been written by qualified and practising practice educators, who have extensive experience not only as practice educators but also in developing and delivering practice education courses.

This book is meant to be a handy guide for all that practice education and working with a student involves. Earlier editions of this book have been much valued, and this edition is written with respect for the previous authors while developing the book to reflect post-pandemic practice education.

The emphasis in this book is on the *application* of the key knowledge and skills which are embedded within the practice educator role; the *what* a practice educator needs to consider within the placement and the *how* of accomplishing it. Many of the theoretical considerations and objectives underpinning practice learning and education and the role of the practice educator that are mentioned in this book are covered in greater detail in other practice education texts, some of which are classics, and we have referred to them in this book. We would encourage you to read these books alongside this one for further insights and ideas, as many of these texts cannot be bettered and remain as relevant to practice education today as when they were initially published.

While aimed primarily at those practice educators who are at the start of their practice educating career, this book will also be helpful for more experienced practice educators, who may view this book as a refresher, and it may be useful for them in considering the requirements of the Professional Capabilities Framework (BASW, 2018), the Knowledge and Skills Statements (DoH, 2015; DfE, 2018) and the PEPS (BASW, 2022) in maintaining and developing their practice.

You may be reading this introduction and overview before reading other chapters in the book, or you may already have dipped into the book and are reading this at a later point. In whatever way you are using this book, this introduction and overview will inform you about the structure of each chapter and provide an explanation of terms used to help your navigation.

Practice education in social work

Practice education in social work in England has been through numerous transformations but is currently subject to the Practice Educator Professional Standards for social work (PEPS) (BASW, 2022). This section reflects on the history and complexity of practice education and will consider the current requirements for social work education, practice education in social work and social work registration. The professional standards outlined below relate to requirements for social work education, training and registration in England. Different requirements exist for the other UK countries.

A brief history of social work education

This section provides a brief historical introduction to social work education to enable an understanding of the foundation of the current social work qualification. While social work education began in social care, students studying social work today need to successfully complete a recognised and ratified social work course (SWE, 2019).

The historical foundations of social work can be traced back to social care, where a dependence on faith-based, class-based and industrial profit-based philanthropists established community-based support (Hill et al, 2018). The first formal social work education appeared within the settlement movement and the Charity Organisation Society (COS), where a series of lectures followed by a one-year university-based course were developed at the beginning of the twentieth century (Burt, 2018; Hill and Frost, 2018). In 1920, Clement Attlee, who prior to entering politics and becoming prime minister was a social worker, wrote a guidance paper on the profession of social work and devoted a chapter to social work training. He recognised that working with an experienced social worker was a positive way to develop social work skills and advocated the importance of a theoretical basis on which to base practice. This was followed by the last of the Younghusband reports (1959), which recommended cohesive national social work training and introduced the two-year social work qualification.

More recently, social work students have been expected to undertake a vocational professional course to qualify them to practise, such as the Certificate of Qualification in Social Work (CQSW) commissioned by the Central Council for Education and Training in Social Work (CCETSW), which ran from 1971 to 1994; the Diploma in Social Work (DipSW) (CCETSW, 1991), which ran from 1992; and the introduction of the social work degree with a greater focus on practice (DoH, 2002), which is the current route to social work qualification and can be offered at either undergraduate or Master's level. Finally, the recent initiative of fast-track social work courses for postgraduate students and apprenticeship routes that enable employed students to have time both in the university and in the workplace have been developed. All routes require the social work student to undertake the requisite number of placement days with a practice educator providing social work supervision and ultimately lead to the status of qualified social worker, with social work's new governing body, Social Work England (SWE), providing guidance in qualifying education and training standards (QETS) (SWE, 2019).

The introduction of the social work degree also saw the introduction of the National Occupational Standards (DoH, 2002), the first of a number of practice standards that social work students have been expected to meet in an attempt to standardise qualifying practice. Sadly, the profession cannot agree on the content of such standards and there are currently multiple frameworks against which universities have to map their courses: the Professional Capabilities Framework (PCF) (BASW, 2018), two Knowledge and Skills Statements (KSS) (DoH, 2015; DfE, 2018) and Social Work England's Professional Standards. Furthermore, for those students undertaking a social work apprenticeship, Knowledge, Skills and Behaviours (KSBs) (IATE, 2018) are also applied. While a joint statement was published to try to link the PCF and KSS standards (BASW, 2018), the situation remains conflicting and confusing for practice educators and social work students, leading to a shift away from the ongoing desire for consistency in social work education (Younghusband, 1959; Croisdale-Appleby, 2014; Narey, 2014).

In the early 2010s, two significant reports were commissioned and published on social work education (Croisdale-Appleby, 2014; Narey, 2014), both of which highlighted that the quality of both academic teaching and practical learning were critical for the development of the requisite knowledge and skills for the future provision of a quality social work service. This led to the Children and Social Work Act 2017 (section 46), which gives universities a duty to deliver '*adequate*' training for social work students. Furthermore, the development of teaching partnerships in 2016 provided a driver for good-quality social work placements, together with a professional commitment to practice education and the development of social work students' knowledge, values and skills. Social work teaching partnerships have seen local universities and social work service providers work together to ensure that social work education is relevant to service provision needs and that placements are of a high quality for all social work students.

Irrespective of these changes in social work education, the consistent theme has been the centrality of the placement, where academic teaching is applied to practice in a supported social work environment. The social work student must experience two contrasting placements, often interpreted as one in adult service provision and one in children's service provision, with at least one enabling the student to undertake statutory duties (SWE, 2019) to prepare them for qualified practice. While on placement, the social work student should be supported by a qualified and registered social worker who is a qualified or qualifying practice educator (SWE, 2019). In order to promote the quality of social work placements, a mandatory practice educator qualification, the PEPS was developed by the now defunct The College of Social Work (TCSW) in 2013, but has been adopted, reviewed and updated by the British Association of Social Workers (BASW, 2022).

As social work education has evolved, so too has the terminology used within practice education in social work. The term *'student supervisor'* was replaced by *'practice teacher'* and an enhanced educational purpose to the role was designated within the requirements of the Practice Teacher Award (CCETSW, 1989); later, the term *'practice assessor'* was introduced and used with the introduction of the social work degree (DoH, 2002). The Practice Teacher Award was replaced by the revised Post Qualification Framework (GSCC, 2005) which included post-qualifying awards at different levels of specialism. The first *'specialist'* level incorporated a module in *'enabling others'*, which required candidates to develop knowledge and skills in enabling the learning and development of others. The introduction of the PEPS in 2013 by BASW promoted practice education as a *'stand-alone'* status and achievement, thus giving the role the prominence and recognition it deserved. The PEPS terminology of practice educator is used throughout this book. Nevertheless, it is helpful here to note that off-site practice educator (OSPE) and on-site supervisor (OSS) are also used within the PEPS to recognise where a placement provides learning opportunities and is supported by an external off-site practice educator.

The Practice Educator Professional Standards for social work (PEPS) (BASW, 2022)

It is expected that all practice educators supporting a student on a social work placement are qualified social workers who are PEPS qualified or are working towards the PEPS qualification. The PEPS are a national minimum requirement for practice educators, and outline two stages of professional development and progression. The two stages are described by BASW (2022) as:

> » *Stage 1 Practice educators at this stage will be able to supervise, teach and assess social work degree students up to, but not being solely responsible for, the final assessment prior to qualification. Stage 1 practice educators supervising final placement students will need to have their decision ratified and overseen by a PEPS 2 qualified practice educator mentor or assessor.*

> » *Stage 2 Practice educators at this stage will be able to supervise, teach and assess social work degree students up to and including the last placement. These practice educators will have the authority to recommend, based on appropriate evidence, that social work learners are fit to practise at the point of qualification.*

The PEPS (BASW, 2022) define the knowledge, skills and values that practice educators need to demonstrate at Stages 1 and 2, and which are outlined within Domains A–D and the Values for Practice Educators and Supervisors. Local and regional partnerships can decide how practice educators can demonstrate and meet the domain requirements and learning outcomes outlined at each stage. The link to the PEPS guidance can be found at the end of this chapter. There must be guidance and support available to practice educators who are undertaking Stages 1 and 2 from an appropriately qualified mentor (who must be Stage 2 qualified). When undertaking Stage 1 and Stage 2, practice educators must also be observed in their practice with a student teaching, supervising and assessing against the PCF (BASW, 2018), and this must be carried out by a Stage 2 qualified and registered social worker.

Social Work England

In December 2019, Social Work England took responsibility for the registration of social workers and the development of the profession. All qualified social workers must be registered with Social Work England in order to be able to practise and ensure that they meet annual CPD requirements. As such, all practice educators in England must be registered with Social Work England to be able to practice educate. They provide the Professional Standards (2020) which all social workers and practice educators must adhere to (see the link at the end of this chapter), thus reinforcing the PEPS (BASW, 2022) statement of values.

Contemporary practice education issues

Practice education in social work has a clear professional context and guidance. Nevertheless, there remain different contexts for placement provision. It should be remembered that social work education takes place within a wider context of changing configurations of social care and social work practice and within conditions of austerity, a post-pandemic world and uncertainty for many vulnerable people and social workers. The unsung work of practice educators within a wider historical narrative is not new. In 2005, Young and Burgess, writing about changes and challenges to teaching in higher education, likened the scenario to '*dancing on a moving carpet… and the challenge of mastering new dance steps*' (Young and Burgess, 2005, p 1). This view is very apt when considering practice education and the role and remit of practice educators within the current landscape. The carpet is indeed moving beneath practice educators with varying degrees of fluidity and forcefulness and resulting from the impact of numerous changes. However, rather than having to learn '*new dance steps*', the role of the practice educator remains the same: to assist the student in creating a sense of the professional self in the social worker role, regardless of programme delivery structure, setting, location or role destination of the student.

It remains as relevant as ever that practice educators play an important part in helping to develop the next generation of social workers and the aim of this book is to assist practice educators in this task. Practice educators bring knowledge, skills and experience to the role through supervision, skill facilitation, case management, teaching and assessment. It is this that enables students to develop social work knowledge and skills so that they can practice effectively and efficiently, working according to the professional standards expected within the profession (SWE, 2019).

This section introduces the collaborative supervisory relationship, social work values, involvement of people with lived experience, and the impact of the Covid-19 pandemic on practice education. These themes will be incorporated throughout the book.

Collaborative supervisory relationship

The term 'supervisory relationship' is used throughout this book to denote the relationship between practice educator and student throughout the placement, not just within social work student supervision. The quality of the supervisory relationship between practice educator and student is a key factor for success in the development of social work knowledge and skills (Roulston et al, 2018; Ketner et al, 2017; Yeung et al, 2021; Beesley, 2022). Research has identified that the supervisory relationship engages students when it is comfortable, supportive, open and honest, accommodating, and friendly with professional boundaries applied, which enables a collaborative approach through which knowledge and skills can be developed (Beesley, 2022). However, there are some challenges in establishing a suitable climate where learners feel comfortable enough that they are willing to be challenged about their assumptions and also confident enough to explore new ways of thinking.

Social work values

Social work values underpin all work undertaken and are required to ensure professionalism. Practice education is no different and has its own statement of values.

PEPS (BASW, 2022) Values Statement of Practice Education

1. *Advise learners of their rights and actively lead on challenging oppression, discrimination and racist practices that may be experienced by learners. This may include overt expressions of racism, or more covert unconscious bias and microaggressions. Learners must be supported throughout the process by the learning provider and (Trainee) Practice Educator in the reporting and responding to such concerns. Where appropriate this will require the implementation of whistleblowing policies (BASW, 2014) to ensure an effective working environment for social work.*

2. *Manage professional and personal boundaries, appropriately using authority and power within the assessment relationship and recognising and acting upon the implications for assessment of practice. Fundamental to this relationship is an underpinning of the common principles of equality, diversity and inclusion in appropriately supporting learners by acknowledging and responding to their needs in an anti-discriminatory manner.*

3. *Update on best practice in assessment and research on adult learning and apply this knowledge in promoting the rights and choices of a diverse group of learners. Managing the assessment process whilst actively challenging oppressive practice which does not support learners to reach their potential.*

4. *Commit to the needs and interests of people with lived experience of social work when assessing the capability and skills of learners at all stages of the assessment process. As appropriate, those with lived experience should play an active part in assessing those being accepted onto and undertaking training in practice education.*

5. *Identify and question their own values and prejudices and respect, value and celebrate the uniqueness and diversity of learners such as those from different entry routes and with different personal and professional experiences. Actively challenge when oppressive practice is observed or reported. This is in line with the Professional Capabilities Framework (BASW 2018, PCF Domain 3).*

6. *Accept and respect learners' circumstances, understand how these impact on the learning and assessment process and make reasonable adjustments as required. Those involved in practice education should recognise and build on learners' strengths and consider individual learning styles and use a range of assessment methods (including those preferred by the learner).*

7. *Implement an holistic approach to assess in a manner that does not stigmatise or disadvantage learners and ensures equality of opportunity in line with the Equality Act 2010. Ensure that the views of those who have lived experiences of social work are central to this assessment process. Show applied knowledge and understanding of the significance of lived experience,*

poverty, racism, ill health, disability, sex, social class, age, gender reassign-
ment, being married or in a civil partnership, being pregnant or on maternity
leave, religion or belief and sexual orientation in managing the assessment
process. Recognise and work to prevent and counter unjustifiable oppression,
discrimination and disadvantage in all aspects of the assessment process. Be
aware of the impact of poverty and associated issues such as food insecurity
and how this might affect the experiences of learners and those accessing
social work services.

8. *Take responsibility for the quality of their work and ensure that it is monitored*
   and appraised; critically reflect on their own practice and identify develop-
   ment needs in order to improve their own performance, raise standards, and
   contribute to the learning and development of others.

(PEPS, BASW, 2022, pp 6–7)

Involvement of people with lived experience

While recognising that the term 'service user' is not always appropriate as it reflects the power differential between a person who uses services and the social worker as service provider, it is used where appropriate within this book to reflect where a student is the service provider. Generally speaking, however, the authors agree that the term 'person with lived experience' is most appropriately used to denote a person who uses services.

Explicit calls to involve people with lived experience in a meaningful fashion have been crucial to recent developments in social work education. A review of the participation of people with lived experience in social work education (Wallcraft et al, 2012) found that, although many universities had well-established partnerships with service users and carers as people with lived experience, there was little evidence of the impact of this on students' practice. It is imperative that practice educators consider their approach to ensure that placements maximise opportunities for students to learn alongside people with lived experience and receive their feedback. Calvin Thomas (2014) offers excellent guidance on how to involve people with lived experience in student placements and their work is referred to throughout this book.

The book will address the involvement of people with lived experience at all stages of practice education, and the practice educator is encouraged to critically reflect on and develop ways in which people with lived experience can be more involved in the student's development of knowledge and skills.

Furthermore, the practice educator has a responsibility to help the student make connections between the learning environment and service delivery. It is hard sometimes for students to understand that while their needs as learners are important, it is the needs of the people who use the services that are paramount. On occasion, the practice educator may have to put the service user's needs before the student's right to a learning opportunity, be that to safeguard a vulnerable person or to respect their wishes, feelings and choices. However, a clear explanation of this prioritisation of the person's rights will support the student's understanding of the rights of vulnerable people and the norms and values of the organisation.

Post-pandemic practice education in social work

The world was turned upside down in early 2020, when the Covid-19 pandemic swept across the globe and impacted every person's life in significant ways. For social work students on placement, this created initial confusion about placement security, followed by a range of responses that included terminating, suspending, shortening or adapting placements to reflect the needs of the students and placement providers. Variations across universities continued, but as the world adjusted to a 'new normal', practice education developed creative and flexible responses to supporting students to develop social work knowledge and skills (Beesley, 2022).

The first significant change that has been evidenced in relation to placement provision is a shift from office-based placement to a more blended location approach. Historically, students were not encouraged to work from home while on placement: this seemed to stem from an apparently unfounded lack of trust that students would engage with placement tasks during this time and, more significantly, that work-based learning should be in the workplace. This thinking was challenged in March 2020, and it has subsequently been proven that students can work and learn from home while on placement. Furthermore, the return to the office has been to a changed landscape, with many local authorities recognising that blended location working and hot-desking are viable, which has enabled a reduction in office space and impacted the ability of full-time office-based working for staff and students alike. That is not to say that blended location learning is without its difficulties, but it is now an accepted pattern of placement learning for many social work students. While many placement providers remained, or have returned to, being fully office based, the discussion is not intended to ignore these practices, but to consider where there has been change.

A benefit of home working and learning is reduced travel costs for the student who may be experiencing financial difficulties in a period where living costs have had a considerable impact on student poverty. However, an important proviso to the student working and learning from home is that they are still able to undertake home visits to service users as required. This means that they will still need access to transport, and where the student is located a distance from the placement patch consideration should be given to whether this is viable. For some placements, home visits can be pre-organised on certain days each week, while other placements will require the student to be able to undertake emergency home visits where required. Nevertheless, the student must have a confidential space to work in when working at home, as professionalism and good practice dictates that communications with and about service users are not overheard by family members or housemates.

The second significant change was the profession embracing remote communication. It can be argued that social workers were reluctant to engage with technology (Haynes, 2019); however, the pandemic required everyone to engage with remote communication, primarily the use of video calls, including via Zoom, Skype and Teams (Mishna et al, 2021). While the telephone enables communication, it does not easily facilitate the development of a working relationship and the observation and assessment of service users that is fundamental to the role of social work. Similarly in practice education, the use of video calls, which will hereafter be referred to as remote communication, has been critical to the development of the supervisory relationship and the assessment of the student.

Many practice educators have developed a pattern of a remote daily check-in with the student during the pandemic, and this is good practice to continue where the student and practice educator are not in the office on the same day. The check-in enables the student to reflect on the previous day's work and ask any questions to ensure work is being completed as per placement expectations. It enables the planning of the coming day's work and learning opportunities. It also develops the supervisory relationship which, as discussed in Chapter 5, enables the student to engage more robustly with the learning opportunities, thus ensuring the development of knowledge and skills.

Finally, the student will need a strong internet connection to enable them to work and learn at home as remote communication requires a good connection. However, this is a further expense for the student and clarification should be sought if they can afford it. If the student is unable to provide an adequate internet connection, the practice educator and student should consider whether the student should be office based.

The practice educator's role here is to ensure that they are clear about the placement provider's accepted placement location and advise the student accordingly to ensure that their home working and learning is facilitated. As placement provision has adapted to a 'new normal', so too must the practice educator's role evolve to engage with different practice education styles that have emerged since the pandemic began (Beesley and Taplin, 2023).

Structure of the book

Each chapter follows a similar structure whereby the theory or concepts behind the subject of that chapter is outlined before applying it to the practice educator's role to enable the student's development. This section describes the learning activities and the content of the chapters.

In order to support the reader to develop their practice education knowledge and skills, the book is laid out to include reflective activities to undertake and includes the following features.

>> *Chapter aims*: each chapter indicates the aims for the chapter.

>> *Critical questions*: these critical questions encapsulate some of the challenges, dilemmas and complexities of the practice educator role that a critically reflective practice educator will be asking themselves throughout their reading of the chapter and during their practice.

>> *Professional development prompts*: these are reflective activities that the practice educator can carry out on their own or with a colleague or mentor to enhance their practice education knowledge, skills and values.

>> *Student development exercises*: these are exercises that a practice educator can undertake with a student.

>> *Case example*: for illustrative purposes.

>> *Impact of the pandemic*: reflections on the positive learning for practice education that has arisen as a result of the pandemic.

>> *Taking it further*: this will direct the reader to helpful resources or further reading to enhance development.

Chapter content

Chapter 2 focuses on the planning and preparation for placement that the practice educator is advised to engage in to ensure that the placement, the team and themselves are able to support the student throughout the placement. It also considers the importance of the induction. Developing this further, Chapter 3 reflects on enabling learning, considering some of the key concepts and ideas underpinning learning, issues associated with practice educating social work students, and examples of learning activities that can be undertaken with the student. Chapter 4 focuses on the importance and development of reflective practice and critical reflection, as well as the practice educator's responsibility to develop the student's knowledge, skills and values and understanding of the impact of power and oppression on vulnerable people.

Chapter 5 considers the supervision process, reflecting on models of supervision, supervision processes, and the supervisory relationship and power and collaboration therein. Chapter 6 addresses the practice educator's role as assessor of the student on placement, including concepts of assessment, assessment criteria and assessment processes. Chapter 7 discusses challenges that may arise during the placement and how to address them, followed by discussion on how to support a student where there are significant areas of development. Finally, Chapter 8 reflects on the qualification of the practice educator under PEPS (BASW, 2022).

Finally...

The role of practice educator is both complex and fulfilling, but is not without challenge. There are considerable time constraints placed on you as a practice educator, and it is rare that you will receive caseload adjustment to reflect the additional time spent with your student. However, the joy of supporting a social work student to develop their knowledge and skills, or address areas for development and overcome challenges to facilitate the next generation of social workers, is often cited in practice educator training as the motivation to become a practice educator. As practice educators, the authors of this book take delight in seeing the careers of former students develop and flourish and are keen to encourage them to become practice educators themselves. There is also personal and professional reward as often you will develop as both a social worker and a practice educator through the necessity to discuss theory, debate ethical dilemmas and reflect on practice with your student.

We wish you all the best in the teaching and learning endeavour of practice education, which is our passion!

Taking it further

British Association of Social Workers (BASW) (2018) *Professional Capabilities Framework*. [online] Available at: www.basw.co.uk/social-work-training/professional-capabilities-framework-pcf. The standards in which social workers in England are expected to operate and the criteria that social work students are assessed against.

British Association of Social Workers (BASW) (2021) *Code of Ethics.* [online] Available at: www.basw.co.uk/about-basw/code-ethics. This provides a comprehensive discussion of the definitions of values, ethics and practice principles with a helpful guide to behaviours representing professional ethical practice.

British Association of Social Workers (BASW) (2022) *Practice Educator Professional Standards.* [online] Available at: www.basw.co.uk/social-work-training/practice-educator-professional-standards-peps. The standards in which practice educators in England are expected to operate.

Social Work England (SWE) (2020) *Professional Standards.* [online] Available at: www.socialworkengland.org.uk/standards/professional-standards/. Professional standards by which social workers in England are expected to operate.

Chapter aims

- » To review principles of good practice in preparing and planning for a social work student placement.

- » To consider the involvement of service users and colleagues in the preparation and planning process.

- » To consider how to meet individual student learning needs.

Critical **questions**

- » Who are you as a practitioner, learner and practice educator?

- » How can you prepare for and provide appropriate learning opportunities for a student across the breadth of the placement?

Introduction

This chapter is designed to address the Practice Educator Professional Standards (PEPS) (BASW, 2022) Domain A – '*Work with others to organise an effective learning environment*' – and the statement of values. As with any social work intervention, preparation is the basis for a successful outcome, or, as the popular business and sports adage goes: '*failing to prepare is preparing to fail*'. Preparation for the practice educator begins from the point at which they reflect with their line manager about whether they want to become a practice educator and continues throughout their training and practice as an educator.

Research has identified that social work students associate placement satisfaction with learning and the development of knowledge, skills and values, as a result of effective supervision, reflective discussion and receiving positive reinforcement and constructive feedback (Roulston et al, 2018; Wilson and Flanagan, 2021; Beesley, 2022). This highlights the importance of the practice educator's role within the student's placement, which is best achieved through a proactive and prepared approach.

This chapter considers the preparation and planning that the practice educator must do to facilitate effective learning opportunities. It will reflect on the planning that needs to take place before first meeting the student, followed by preparation of colleagues and people who use services. The chapter then focuses on meeting the student and consider both the informal meeting and the placement learning agreement (PLA) meeting before considering the planning and preparation that the practice educator should undertake to ensure an effective first day of placement and induction. Finally, the chapter considers the planning and preparation required as the placement progresses, including collaborative supervisory relationships, workload allocation, involvement of people with lived experience, placement-related activities and placement endings.

Before meeting the student

Before meeting the student there are a number of critical issues that the practice educator should consider. Firstly, the practice educator will need to undertake preparatory 'internal' reflections that enhance self-awareness and emotional intelligence in relation to their role as a practice educator. In turn this will promote more 'external' reflections for the practice educator, where consideration will be required in relation to the placement organisation and team's learning culture and operational values. Indeed, *'planning and preparation should ideally start at the moment you first consider the possibility of providing support for learning in your workplace'* (Williams and Rutter, 2021, p 30).

This section reflects on practice educator training and preparation of self, followed by preparation that includes colleagues and people who use services.

Practice educator training

Before being able to support their first student on placement, the practice educator must be enrolled on a practice educator training programme. The content of this varies from programme to programme, but in essence it will introduce the placement process, adult learning theories, promotion of the development of the Professional Capabilities Framework (PCF) (BASW, 2018) required core social work skills – including professionalism, values, diversity, critical reflection and knowledge – and assessment strategies. Chapter 8 outlines the PEPS (BASW, 2022), which apply to all practice educators in England and can be usefully read at this stage and as the course progresses. However, before embarking on practice educator training, it is helpful for the social worker to reflect on their motivation for becoming a practice educator.

Professional **development prompt**

> » What are your motivations to become a practice educator?

It is recognised that for some social workers, a qualification in practice education is a requirement to enable them to progress within their social work career, and they may never engage with practice education beyond the qualification. This is a shame, and where that is the case, the practice educator is asked to reflect on whether this impacts on the quality of practice education that they provide to the student. However, when asked about their motivation, many potential practice educators respond that they want to contribute to the next generation of qualified social workers, want to repay their own experience of having had a good practice educator, are orientated in their career towards education or supervision, or that they wanted a new challenge. Any of these reasons are good motivators and will hopefully sustain a social worker through the challenges they might face in becoming a qualified practice educator.

Preparation of self

As part of the practice educator training, the practice educator will be asked to reflect on their readiness to provide a placement for a social work student. It may be helpful to think of preparation in terms of thinking about your social work and practice educator knowledge, skills, values and strengths. Practice educators should remain actively aware of the impact of discrimination and oppression on people who use services and on their own personal and professional values.

Professional **development prompt**

> » What do you see as your core social work values?
> » Do you routinely reflect on your values and the impact they have on your practice?
> » How will you apply them to practice education?

This professional development prompt is designed to ensure that you are aware of your personal and professional values, perhaps taking a step back to think about '*conscious competence*' (Burch, 1970), because continual reflection and consideration of values is the only way to engage actively in anti-discriminatory and anti-oppressive practice. Indeed, the practice educator must be mindful of their own values in order to be able to promote them with the student, and thus to be able to assess the student's development of social work values. In addition, the practice educator must reflect on the power that derives from the role of practice educator and how this power should be used to motivate the student to engage with learning activities rather than to demotivate them. Finally, the practice educator is required to ensure that people who use services are not oppressed by the student's need to develop social work knowledge and skills.

The PEPS Values Statement – Practice Education (BASW, 2022) – as set out in Chapter 1 – is a robust and complex list that requires the practice educator to spend some time reading, absorbing and reflecting upon. However, the fact that it is robust is an indication of the importance that should be afforded to social work values within practice education. This is appropriate because not only do practice educators have to practise professionally in supporting a student, but they also have to be mindful of the needs of people who use services and with whom the student will develop their knowledge and skills. The practice educator must be self-aware to be able to practice educate in a facilitative and collaborative manner (Beesley, 2022) and thus reflection on self, the power held in the role and student-centred practice are all important.

It is impossible to talk about practice education without referencing the inherent power dynamic between practice educator and student. As we have said, power can be used positively through collaboration and empowerment to motivate the student to engage with learning activities and supervision, or it can be used to control learning and to devalue a student. Preparation of self for practice education must include reflection on your role and the power afforded therewithin.

Wonnacott (2012) used the term '*authoritative*' as the ideal style of the effective practice educator; an authoritative supervisor being clear about expectations and practice standards but also able to work effectively with relationships and provide a safe and enabling environment. An authoritative practice educator should collaborate with the student to ensure that the student feels valued and supported, and yet is able to facilitate appropriate challenge.

Professional **development prompt**

» How do you practice educate authoritatively? How do you empower the student to be engaged in their own learning?

» Are there ways in which you could enhance your practice education practice to value the student further?

» How do you think that your student perceives you? Ask them for feedback on your strengths and areas for development: do they align with your perception of yourself?

There is a potential for misuse and abuse of power within a supervisory relationship or it can be used positively to motivate development (Kadushin and Harkness, 2014). In order to develop an understanding of the influence of social power on motivation, French and Raven (1959) provided five classifications of power, which remain pertinent: legitimate, expert, referent, reward and coercive power. They argued that it is social power, that is, how authority is used, that influences the recipient and impacts the development of knowledge and skills. The practice educator's legitimate and expert power can be used to the student's detriment; for example, an overly authoritarian approach can instil fear and demotivate (Leung, 2012; Kadushin and Harkness, 2014; Beddoe, 2017). However, it can also be used to empower, such as through a collaborative approach that acknowledges power and seeks to share it with students to motivate and engage (Hair, 2014; Egan et al, 2017). By contrast, reward power (French and Raven, 1959) is the provision of a perceived outcome, which can occur by means of a practical, emotional or developmental reward. Finally, coercive power (French and Raven, 1959) can be demotivating if areas for development are used as a punishment through threats, such as the placement being considered unsuccessful (Kadushin and Harkness, 2014). Nevertheless, that does not mean that raising concerns about practice should be avoided, and practice educators should be assertive and clear in the need to make decisive placement outcome decisions where required (Finch, 2017) – this will be discussed in Chapter 7.

Developing French and Raven's classifications of power, Brown and Bourne (1996) suggest that the supervisory relationship is influenced by two types of power: formal and informal power. Within the supervisory relationship, the practice educator has formal power and authority embedded in the role as they are the ultimate assessor of the student and it is their holistic assessment of the student, based on their professional judgement, which will determine whether the student passes or fails the placement. Informal power is that which derives from the practice educator's personal attributes and their professional knowledge and skills and status as a qualified social worker. Such structural determinants of informal power – and the hidden assumptions or unspoken manifestations that can apply as a result of them – can exert a powerful influence on the placement and the supervision process, and the practice educator needs to think about and recognise where they may be apparent. It is also important to consider the influence that factors such as institutional racism may have on both practice educator and student (Tedam, 2021).

Furthermore, Davys and Beddoe (2009) note that there can be barriers to the exploration of ideas and feelings within supervision that can stem from three fears, which they characterise as fear of being overwhelmed by feelings; fear of the judgement of others; and fear of distortion within the professional encounter. It is worthwhile considering how these fears and barriers to the exploration of emotions may be manifested in the placement setting – for both students and practice educators – and how they might be managed. For the student, emotional feelings may be perceived as adding to anxiety or pressure already associated with the placement, and they may be suppressed in favour of a desire to simply *get on with the placement and pass*. Feelings may be perceived by students as a sign of weakness or, being conscious of the value base of social work, they may feel uncomfortable about sharing strong negative feelings about vulnerable people or their lifestyles, believing that if they do this, they or their practice will be judged adversely. Students are also acutely aware that they are being assessed on placement and can avoid mentioning anything that would suggest they may be struggling with any aspect of practice or professional development.

The practice educator will need to reflect upon and acknowledge the potential power differentials within the placement and the supervisory relationship as part of their preparation for the placement. It is helpful to invite a discussion of power at an early stage of the placement, and certainly when discussing the supervision agreement, which will involve being explicit about the manner in which power and authority will be used. To practise in the role with social work values at heart, the practice educator will need to maintain a continued awareness of the impact of structural oppression and power differentials and demonstrate a willingness to listen, to respond to feedback from the student, to collaborate, and to ensure the relationship is underpinned by openness and honesty. It can be helpful to reflect on areas that might challenge you and how you will address them. The following is one possible scenario.

Professional **development prompt**

>> Your student shares that she and her female partner have decided to get married in a few weeks' time and shares with you that she will need time off placement for her hen trip, wedding and honeymoon.

>> What values are challenged here?

Here you are in a powerful position: ultimately, you can determine if the wedding goes ahead or not. The first value that may be challenged is the right for same-sex marriages, which is legal and ethical, but remains against some religious and cultural values but not social work values. The second value that might be challenged is the student's orientation to learning (Knowles, 1973) and her work ethic, where you may feel that she should be prioritising her placement and that her placement learning will be disrupted by multiple periods of time off. Conversely, your personal values may be romantically orientated, and you give your blessing without any reflection. This is an ethical dilemma, and your decision making would be based not only on your own values, but also on the policies and procedures of your agency and the student's education provider. This professional development prompt is not designed to prompt a correct decision, but to stimulate your thinking about your social work values when supporting a student.

Practical preparation

The role of practice educator is both complex and straightforward. The practice educator has responsibility to:

>> attend all placement meetings;

>> provide learning opportunities for the student;

>> liaise with all other involved parties, including colleagues;

>> provide weekly supervision;

>> provide informal support to the student between supervision sessions;

>> undertake direct observations of practice;

>> provide timely and constructive feedback;

>> write the interim and final reports;

>> make a final recommendation of pass or fail in relation to the student's development against the appropriate level of the Professional Capabilities Framework (BASW, 2018).

On a purely practical level, the practice educator needs to ensure that their own workload is planned and organised in a way which is conducive to hosting a social work student placement. If the practice educator works on a part-time basis or has a flexible working pattern, they will need to think about their time management and maintaining accountability and availability for their student. While some placement providers have an agreement for workload relief for practice educators when they are hosting a placement, many do not. Furthermore, it is helpful for the practice educator to explore the support that may be available to them as a practice educator, such as practice educator support groups, peer support or mentor support.

Finally, it is vital that the practice educator develops a working knowledge of the relevant social work course requirements, including the start date and length of placement, days to be on placement and the framework for the assessment of placements. It is worth noting that different social work education providers, and even different courses within the same university, have different forms and expectations. The practice educator should ensure that they have received information from the education provider as to their documentation, assessment requirements, procedural structures and expectations of practice educators, which may come in paper or electronic handbook format, before the placement begins.

Professional **development prompt**

Reflect on what you can draw on from your role as a social worker to help you develop skills in enabling learning that will apply to a student. Consider your strengths in relation to:

» organisational skills;

» engaging people, including service users, colleagues and other professionals;

» working in a person-centred manner;

» supporting vulnerable people to access services and develop skills;

» assessing strengths and areas for development;

» providing constructive feedback where there are areas of concern.

All of these are transferable skills that will set you in good stead when acting as a practice educator for a social work student. A further word of encouragement is that your line manager would not have nominated you for the practice educator training if they did not feel that you had the skills and temperament to become a practice educator. It can also be helpful to reflect on your learning style and teaching style, both of which are discussed in Chapter 3.

Finally, the practice educator needs to liaise with colleagues within the team and externally to the team to ensure that an appropriate learning space is prepared for the student, including allocation of desk space or arrangements for hot-desking, a computer or laptop identified and an IT log-in organised. These are more important where a blended placement is proposed to enable the student to work effectively from home. The practice educator should liaise with the placement co-ordinator and/or training department to identify any mandatory training that should be pre-booked to occur within the induction period and any optional training choices that can also be presented to the student.

Preparation of colleagues

The practice educator's personal preparation is only one of the key aspects of preparation for a student, another being to prepare colleagues and the wider team. While the practice educator has final responsibility for the student's learning opportunities, this can and should include the facilitation of their learning in the team setting. The practice educator should talk to colleagues beforehand, with a view to involving them in teaching sessions, shadowing opportunities, joint working and assessment opportunities, as students need access to a varied skill mix and a community of practice (Lave and Wenger, 1991). However, as Williams and Rutter (2021) discuss, the practice educator cannot naively assume all members of a team will feel positively towards a student. Previous negative experiences may influence the reception of another student; current issues, including increased stress and workloads, within workplaces and organisations may lead to anxiety and a reluctance to host a student placement. Nevertheless, it can be helpful to place the student's arrival on the team meeting agenda to ensure all colleagues are aware of the placement start date and to reiterate the usefulness of team and individual colleague support.

The environment in which the student learns is one of the singularly most important elements of the placement as it may fundamentally affect the success or otherwise of the learning experience. Of course, the word 'environment' does not relate solely to the physical aspects, although these are important, but also to the culture within the team and organisation. It may be beyond the control of the practice educator to ensure that the placement operates within an organisation that promotes reflective practice and supervision, although it is hoped that this exists. However, discussion in team meetings with the line manager and colleagues can help to promote a positive learning environment that nurtures not just the student's development, but also the development of the whole team. Where reflective, and sometimes boisterous, discussions occur in team rooms that debate constructively how a social worker can enhance practice, the student is provided with modelling on the importance of debate.

Similarly, the practice educator cannot change the composition and identity of the team, but they can reflect on where there are similarities and differences in personalities and ways of working, both within the team and with the student. Social work is predominantly undertaken by women, and male students can feel less able to engage with learning opportunities in a predominantly female placement team (Furness, 2012). Students from a Black and global minority heritage also report feeling alienated within predominantly white-British placement teams (Fairtlough et al, 2014). This clearly raises the need for the practice educator to reflect on whether the team identity may have a negative impact on the student's ability to engage with learning opportunities.

Case **example**

An example of alienation once reported by a student to the authors was that she was often invited by team members to join them for a drink after work. However, the student was Muslim and felt that this was not inclusive and that it demonstrated an ignorance of her personal beliefs. She reported that the practice educator feedback to her was that she was not a 'team-player' as she did not socialise with the team, which alienated her further. She felt that the team were judging her and withdrew from informal team discussions and social interactions, which resulted in colleagues becoming reluctant to invite her on joint visits. Consequently, the practice educator did not feel that the student was engaging with the learning opportunities and an action plan was proposed. The downward spiral of lack of expectation and isolation had a negative impact on the student's self-esteem and self-confidence.

By taking a culturally sensitive approach to socialising, this scenario could have been avoided. The reader is asked to reflect on team norms to consider if they are inclusive *before* the placement begins so that they can take preventative rather than reactive action, reflecting on the impact of the team on the student. However, the reader should also use critical race theory to reflect on whether the student had inadvertently confirmed the practice educator and team's unconscious racial bias that the student would not socialise because she was Muslim, using a socially constructed deficit lens (Tedam, 2021).

Finally, it can be helpful for the practice educator to reflect on how the team deals with conflict. In the case example, the team abandoned the student rather than engaging in discussion to resolve the perceived problem. However, it is not unusual for teams to have other unhealthy conflict management strategies, such as creating an *'us and them'* situation within the team or with the manager that results in gossip and tension, uncomfortable silences or loud disagreements. If you recognise any of these within your team, the question should be firstly: is it safe or appropriate for a student to have a placement in this team and secondly, does the team need external relationship-building support?

Professional **development prompt**

> » What features identify your team as a positive learning environment? Create a list and order them in terms of significance.

> » Ask a colleague to do the same: do you share a similar view?

> » Can you identify anything that could enhance the team's learning environment?

Sometimes we take for granted that we are an *'open'* team or a *'welcoming'* team, but reflecting on what makes the team appear that way and identifying any norms or expectations can support our preparation for the student's arrival. An equally helpful exercise is asking the student to undertake this task partway through their placement (or at the end, if you feel it will give you a more honest answer) to gather feedback on how it feels coming into the team: this feedback can then be applied to enhance the experience of future students.

Preparation of service users

At the preparation stage, people who use services should be informed that a student is joining the team and be asked if they agree to a student social worker being allocated to them; they could also be asked to create a short piece of writing, or audio or video, introducing themselves to the student (Calvin Thomas, 2014). However, you may be able to think of other ways in which as the practice educator you can facilitate the involvement of people with lived experience in both the teaching and assessment of students on placement.

Meeting the student

Initially, the practice educator will receive written details of a prospective student from their agency placement co-ordinator or directly from the social work education provider; these details are often confirmed in a placement application form (PAF), which should include a synopsis of the student's previous experience and learning needs. While the PAF may include details of any reasonable adjustments required in relation to additional learning or health needs, these details may equally not be shared until the first meeting with the student, as the student has the right to choose when, or even if, they share this information with the practice educator. The practice educator is thus likely to begin to assess the student's abilities and learning before meeting them, and it is important to remember that a non-judgemental approach should be taken to ensure assumptions are not made. Where the practice educator becomes aware that reasonable adjustments may be necessary, they should liaise with the placement co-ordinator, education provider and student to ensure that the student's needs are met within the placement environment in accordance with agency procedures.

Meeting the student for the first time can provoke anxiety for both the practice educator and the student. For the practice educator, it is a first chance to meet the student and get a sense of how they will fit within the team, while for the student, they are likely to feel anxious at the prospect of being assessed and evaluated. It may be helpful to have two pre-placement meetings: an informal introductory meeting and a more formal placement learning agreement (PLA) meeting.

While these meetings can take place using remote communication, it has been found preferable if they are undertaken in the agency itself (Beesley and Taplin, 2023), as it enables the supervisory relationship to begin to develop and allows for preliminary assessment of the student by the practice educator and for the student to get a clear sense of the placement. That said, it is not unusual for the tutor and mentor, where appropriate, to join the PLA meeting remotely.

Informal meeting

The opportunity to meet the student on an informal basis is an important part of establishing the supervisory relationship. This is where the student attends the agency to meet the practice educator, providing an opportunity for initial introductions to the workplace and the team. It is important here that the line manager does not become overly involved other than being introduced as a colleague; otherwise, there is a danger that the informal meeting can become a more formal initial assessment. It can be helpful to prepare a few questions to ask the student in order to ensure that they are orientated to the available learning opportunities at the agency (Knowles, 1973). Similarly, it is likely that the student will have prepared some questions to support their understanding of placement expectations. It can be helpful for the practice educator to provide pre-placement reading in the form of a folder of information or direction to helpful websites about the work of the agency or the theoretical principles that underpin the work of the team.

The purpose of the informal meeting is for the practice educator and the student to identify the needs, concerns and interests of the student, and to agree on whether suitable learning opportunities are available for the student to demonstrate their capability. Issues of reasonable adjustment should be clearly discussed. In most cases, this goes well, and the placement is agreed. However, on occasion there will be a reason that the placement may not be able to proceed. This may be for practical reasons, for example, if the student and the practice educator attend the same place of worship; or it could relate to the presentation of the student, if they were late or appeared disinterested; or because specific learning needs cannot be met. If this occurs, it is essential that the practice educator provides clear feedback to the student and relevant placement co-ordinator, as it may be that further discussion may enable the placement to go ahead.

Placement learning agreement meeting

Following the informal meeting, it is the student's responsibility to organise the PLA meeting. This can be a difficult task and should be initiated as soon as there is agreement that the placement is viable. The student, practice educator and the student's personal tutor or other representative from the education provider should be present; however, where a mentor and/or on-site supervisor (OSS) are involved, they should also be present. It should be held at the placement location where possible and before the student starts their placement. Preparation by the practice educator for the PLA meeting should include reflection on available learning opportunities so that they are ready to contribute during the meeting.

The PLA meeting should be chaired by the tutor and the student should complete the PLA form as a record of the proceedings. The meeting will clarify each participant's details and roles, address practical placement details and reasonable adjustments, and discuss the student's learning needs and the placement's learning opportunities. It is helpful for the practice educator to agree arrangements for the first day at the end of the PLA meeting with the student. The PLA form should be completed and distributed for verification and signature by all parties within the first two weeks of the placement; the completion of this task can be considered an early indication of the student's professionalism.

The PLA meeting and subsequent written record are very important as they create and record the expectations for the placement and can be referred to at any stage in the placement if any of the participants feel that the agreement is not being adhered to. All too often the PLA form is completed and put away only to resurface at the end of placement when it is added to the placement portfolio. However, good practice dictates that the practice educator refers to the learning needs recorded in the PLA regularly within social work student supervision, ensuring that the learning needs continue to be congruent with the available learning opportunities and assessing the student's development against the learning needs.

The placement begins

The first weeks of placement are often long awaited and anticipated by practice educator and social work student alike, and it is important that they are well-organised as they set the tone for the rest of the placement. This section reflects on the first day of the placement, blended placement provision and the induction period, and how the practice educator can prepare to enhance their effectiveness.

The arrival of the student

On the first day of the placement, the practice educator should ensure that they are present in the agency and available to the student. Being present is a mark of respect and of placing the student's experience above the day-to-day demands of workload pressures on that special day. If possible, ensure that the student has an identified desk; this further values the student as it immediately provides a message of welcome and of being wanted.

Case **example**

Hilary and Heather are two students who started placements on the same day and afterwards met to compare experiences.

Hilary had been told to go into placement a little after 9.30am to let her practice educator arrive before her and was welcomed with a new mug and an allocated desk. The practice educator had a clear plan for the day, which included planning for the rest of the week. Hilary was very excited as she had already been asked to ring some other agencies. She was tired at the end of the day because she had been given a lot of information to process but felt really positive that the placement would be excellent.

> *Heather arrived at the placement on time, but her practice educator did not arrive until 10am, apologising that she had been on a visit on the way to the office. In fact, Heather had little else to say about her first day as she felt she was given a pile of information to wade through and left to find somewhere to read. She wasn't sure if she wanted to go back the next day but hoped it would be better then.*

Differences are immediately apparent between the two students' experiences and the impact that the day had on them. It is likely that you would prefer to be Hilary's practice educator than Heather's and would be mortified if your student reflected in this way on their first day. When the practice educator has a plan of activities for the first day of placement, it provides structure for the student, as students often reflect on not knowing what to do at first. The first-day activities should include introducing the student to the team: an office desk plan with names on can help with this, as well as an introduction to team culture, such as if there is a coffee fund and where team members usually take their lunch break. There will be other important things that need to be explained, including toilet location and fire evacuation procedures. The practice educator should make time to reflect with the student on the plan for their induction, so that expectations are clear and planned activities can be adjusted to meet any student-led requests. Finally, it is good to be kind to the student on the first day; an early finish that addresses the likelihood of information overload being emotionally tiring is often appreciated.

It is important to recognise that the student is likely to be anxious attending the placement on the first day, and that this anxiety may present itself in different ways: for example, as quietness, over-confident loudness or even shortness of temper. Preparatory empathy (Shulman, 1993) is important for the practice educator here, as understanding the student's initial responses to a stressful situation can enable both diagnostic assessment of the student and the ability to support the student appropriately on the day and as the placement progresses.

Blended placement provision

Impact of the pandemic

As a result of the pandemic, many placements are now operating as blended placements, where the student is facilitated to work both in the office and at home, in addition to undertaking a blend of face-to-face interventions and remote communications.

Facilitating the student's home working and learning raises the issue of confidentiality, which is a core social work value. The student will require a place to work within their home that enables them to talk confidentially about and to service users where family members and/or housemates cannot overhear them. While many workers sat at kitchen tables or balanced laptops on their knees on a sofa or bed during the pandemic and fought for a quiet space to work, for social workers and social work students a confidential space is a non-negotiable requirement. Post-pandemic, students may find themselves sharing accommodation where a family member or housemate is also working at home or is at home for other reasons. As such, the student will need to consider where they are locating themselves to work and learn from home. If the student is unable to find a confidential space within their home, the student and practice educator will need to negotiate to see if a completely office-based placement is viable.

A practice educator also needs to be mindful of a student's ability to support their own children while on placement. The school day is generally shorter than the working day of a social worker, and children will have school holidays and periods of sickness when they cannot attend school. While older children may be able to be independent within the home, where there are younger children at home and for children under school age, the student should ensure that they do not have responsibility to care for them during the placement day to enable them to focus on the placement work and learning. Arrangements can often be made to accommodate childcare, but it is important that this is discussed and agreed, if possible, before the placement starts or certainly in its early stages.

Finally, agreement over the use of a laptop and storage of any paperwork is critical for students who are working and learning from home. All placement work must be undertaken on an agency laptop to ensure confidentiality, and there are usually further security checks such as a password and/or daily remote verification. The laptop should be stored in a locked cupboard or filing cabinet, as should any paperwork that the student has. This should be addressed in the PLA meeting and should be reiterated and recorded in the first supervision session to ensure that the student is clear about this expectation, as not doing so would raise an area for development in relation to professionalism.

The practice educator's role here is to ensure that the student understands the expectations of working at home and confirms that they are home working and learning in a confidential space.

Professional **development prompt**

» How do you ensure that the student has a confidential space when working and learning at home?

» What support do you need to give to a student to enable them to work and learn at home effectively?

Induction

Induction usually takes place in the first two weeks of the placement, although this should be flexible to meet the student's learning pace and any outstanding learning which may be necessary as the placement progresses. The induction period is a time when the student is closely supported by the practice educator to develop a clear understanding of the placement environment. In planning the induction, it is important to take account of the student's individual needs, confidence and interests: this information is best obtained in the informal meeting and PLA meeting before the placement begins but can be adjusted as the induction progresses. Good placement planning and a thorough induction will help the student to feel welcome, to become familiar with the requirements of their role, and to understand the agency's structure and policies. Induction should not be a random series of events; it is a method of learning about the placement organisation and team.

The practice educator should consider what the student needs to know and how this should be paced across the induction period, and should remember to ensure that there is time each day to facilitate student reflection on the induction learning activities. The induction programme should be varied to include different activities throughout each day and across the two weeks, as learners may find it difficult to focus on the same learning exercise for extended periods. Figure 2.1 provides a link between the different ways people learn and induction activities. VARK (Fleming, 2001) stands for visual, aural, reading/writing and kinaesthetic learning. Figure 2.1 shows that induction learning should take account of all four styles of learning to create a multi-modal induction programme that is varied and engaging for the student.

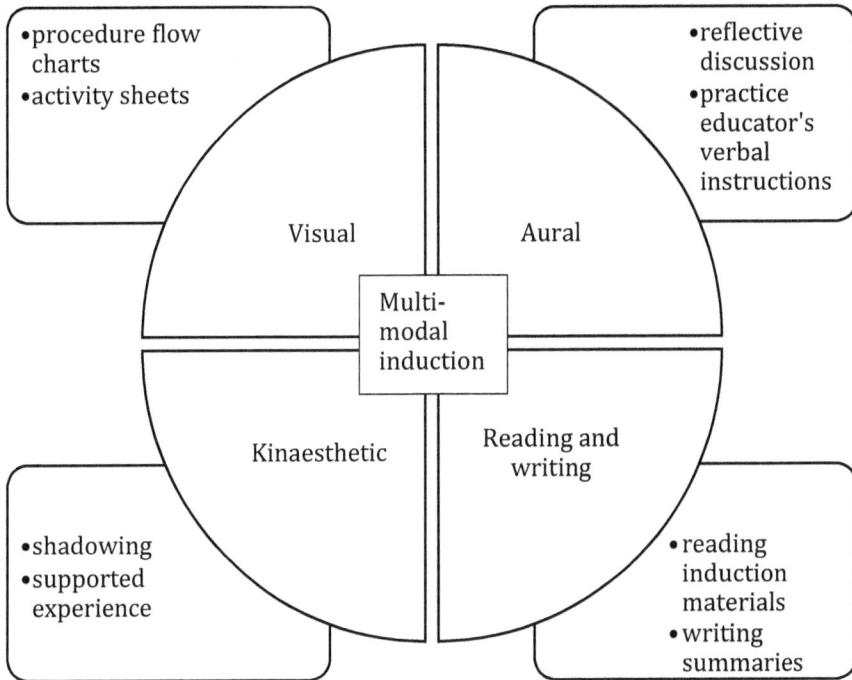

Figure 2.1 Adapted from the VARK (Fleming, 2001) learning styles model to illustrate induction activities

Induction activities may include:

» daily check-ins to reflect on induction activities;

» weekly supervision, including the establishment of a supervision agreement and expectations of supervision;

» creation of placement ID;

» shadowing the practice educator to familiarise the student with the variety of work available;

» accessing the policies and procedures of the placement;

» shadowing a variety of colleagues to observe different intervention styles;

» visiting other agencies to develop an understanding of the context in which the placement operates;

» reading about relevant theories and models;

» relevant training activities;

» reflection on all induction activities.

A helpful exercise is to plan the induction on a grid representing the initial induction fortnight, which can be shared with the student. This would involve putting in set activities, including pre-booked training events, supervision and team meetings, and organisational induction requirements, such as reading policies and procedures, so that there is a skeletal structure. However, the practice educator would leave blanks for collaborative completion on the first day of placement and subsequent collaborative review. Indeed, it is important to negotiate elements of the induction package with the student as this both empowers the student and takes account of their previous work and educational experiences, both of which should contribute to the early stages of the development of the supervisory relationship. Furthermore, andragogical principles (Knowles, 1973) suggest that students like to be responsible for their own learning; setting them tasks to organise their own induction learning activities can be productive.

Student **development exercise**

> » Provide the student with a list of partner agencies and their contact details and ask the student to make contact by telephone to arrange visits to explore the services they offer.

This is an excellent induction learning activity as it requires the need to use the phone, a skill often avoided by students in the first week of placement; it enables the student to demonstrate skills in organisation, prioritisation, diary management and professionalism and can increase the student's self-confidence if they can see that they have completed a set task early in the placement. Conversely, where the student does not begin the task within the first few days, it facilitates the practice educator's diagnostic assessment and stimulates directed reflective discussion about why the student is avoiding undertaking the task, which in turn can enable the practice educator to support the student to overcome the barriers and engage with the learning activity.

Finally, an important part of reflecting on your practice as a practice educator is to seek feedback from the student on their experiences of the induction. This enables you to reflect on their experiences and adjust the induction of the next student as a result. However, a word of caution: if a student identifies themselves as an '*activist*' and reflects that they just wanted to '*get into it*', this should not prompt you to abandon the required reading; and vice versa where the student is a theorist and reflects that they did not value shadowing colleagues, this should not lead you to abandon that learning activity. Indeed, feedback on the induction is an important part of your evaluation of your practice, which is required as part of your PEPS (BASW, 2022) qualification and should be discussed with your mentor.

Impact of the pandemic

Many practice educators have reflected that it is helpful if the induction is carried out in the placement office as it provides an opportunity for the student to meet the team across the fortnight and for the development of a relationship with the practice educator that can then be built on over the rest of the placement (Beesley and Taplin, 2023). To enable an office-based induction, the practice educator may have to adjust their own work pattern in the short term and may find it helpful to ask team members to identify a day when they can be in the office to support the student and facilitate shadowing opportunities.

It is at this time that the student develops a sense of identity and belonging within the team, and therefore inclusion by the team is critical. It can be helpful to have a team meeting within the induction fortnight, even if it is outside the normal pattern of team meetings. This can be via remote communication, in the office, or even at a social event such as a picnic or coffee morning. In addition, if the team have a WhatsApp group for professional or social communication, try to ensure that the student is invited to this group.

Training is an essential part of induction, and the availability of e-training has increased as a result of the pandemic, making training more accessible for the student. As part of the pre-placement preparation, the practice educator should enrol the student in all relevant e-training opportunities – as well as in-person training courses – for which they are eligible and able to attend.

As the placement progresses

As the student settles into the placement, the practice educator is required to continue to plan and prepare for the different stages of the placement to ensure that the placement facilitates appropriate learning opportunities, engages and offers appropriate challenge to the student, and meets the education provider's procedural requirements and assessment criteria. This next section considers the planning required by the practice educator in relation to workload allocation, involvement of people with lived experience, placement-related activities and placement endings.

Workload allocation

It is the practice educator's role to allocate work to the student. This is a balancing act, as the practice educator wants the student to be challenged and busy but not to be overwhelmed. Indeed, the allocation of workload to the student requires constant fine-tuning and review within supervision, and the practice educator should not be afraid to act in adjusting the number of cases held by the student. The practice educator should prepare for this aspect of their role by being aware of and reflecting upon the mechanisms for allocating appropriate work to the student and what type of work is available. Furthermore, planning with the line manager enables the practice educator to allocate work that meets the organisational needs of the placement and the learning needs of the student, while also being aware of the needs of the service user who is the recipient of the intervention.

The practice educator should consider the type of work to be allocated to the student. A breadth of work should be allocated to maximise the student's learning experience and all work should serve a purpose in meeting their learning needs. A collaborative approach is useful here where the student is asked what type of work they wish to undertake, and whether there are any particular areas of development that they feel they need to address. In addition, the practice educator should consider whether certain tasks will be co-worked or independently worked with supervision, as both types of work develop different skills. The complexity of the work also needs to be considered, as it will depend on the student's existing abilities and should become more complex as the placement continues if the student is able to demonstrate the development of knowledge and skills. Finally, the practice educator can reflect on the allocation of different types of work beyond 'casework', which could include groupwork and project work.

Involvement of people with lived experience

It is right that service users and carers are considered central to the social work student placement, as it is their lives that will be impacted by the student's interventions. The practice educator has a responsibility to help the student make connections between the learning environment and service delivery. The first, and most obvious, way that people with lived experience are involved in the student's placement is that they are the service users with whom the student works. As discussed above, the practice educator is required to prepare service users for working with a student by ensuring that they are enabled to make an informed decision about whether or not they are allocated to the student. Once the student is allocated to work with a service user, the practice educator should prepare the student by ensuring that they understand the importance of stating that they are a social work student and exploring how this may be seen by a potential service user or carer.

Likewise, allocated service user involvement in the placement can go further than informed consent. The practice educator could prepare both the service user and the student to make part of their initial visit a discussion about the service user's experiences of service provision to foster empathic understanding and enhance knowledge and skills.

In addition to the usual opportunities for feedback following direct observations and written feedback gathered by the student, as discussed in Chapter 6, one possible route to more meaningful reflection could be to arrange a separate supervision session wherein the practice educator, service user and student collaborate in a planned discussion focused on adding the service user perspective to an experience. This would provide an opportunity for the student and practice educator to hear the service user's experience first-hand and also – and perhaps just as importantly – to allow the student to test out their own assumptions against reality. This task can boost both the service user's self-confidence and self-esteem and the student's development of knowledge and skills.

Student **development exercise**

» In preparation for a reflective discussion with a service user, ask the student to research materials about the views of people with lived experience on service delivery in your particular area of practice. This could include service user forums or websites, or research published by people with lived experience.

» In a reflective discussion with a service user, ask the student to present their understanding and enable the service user to explore their own experiences of being a service user to develop these ideas further.

This student development exercise is designed to develop the student's empathic understanding of the experiences that people with lived experience may have of social work service provision. A word of caution is that this is only successful where the practice educator has spent time supporting the service user and the student to engage with the activity so that the expectations of the task are clearly set out.

Placement-related activities

The practice educator will be required to undertake a number of placement-related tasks, which include supervision (as discussed in Chapter 5), direct observations, writing interim and final reports and attending placement meetings (as discussed in Chapter 6). Guidance on each of these will be provided by the education provider and should be referred to by the practice educator to reinforce understanding.

Social work student supervision is discussed extensively in Chapter 5 but at this stage it is important to note that planning and preparation for supervision by the practice educator is key. Research has found that where the practice educator takes a diligent approach and is prepared for supervision, it enables constructive feedback, facilitates informed decision making and leads to more efficient and effective practice (Beesley, 2022).

Placement endings

As the student nears the end of the placement, the practice educator still has elements of planning and preparation that they should engage in. The practice educator should plan a supervision activity to support the student in the closure or summary of their work and plan goodbyes. In addition, the practice educator needs to approve, or seek line manager approval for, closures, and facilitate the transfer of outstanding work to either themselves (as is often the case) or back to the line manager, to ensure that work is not lost and final accountability for the student's work is assumed. In addition, the practice educator should take the opportunity to discuss the student's learning needs for future placement or qualified practice with them to support the transition that the student is making. In addition, where the student is completing their final placement, the practice educator can provide support and advice on applying for jobs.

The practice educator may wish to organise a leaving lunch and/or present, and this once again values the student as a member of the team. It is as important for the practice educator to be present at the placement on the last day of placement as it was to be present on the first day and providing an ending for the student is important for both the practice educator and the student.

Conclusion

This chapter has looked closely at the planning and preparation required by the practice educator before and during the placement. More than anything else, this chapter illustrates the importance of preparation at every stage of the student's placement as this is crucial in the development of the student's knowledge and skills.

Taking it further

Turner, D (ed) (2021) *Social Work and Covid-19*. St Albans: Critical Publishing. This is an excellent guide to how the pandemic has affected social work provision with a range of people with lived experience. Chapter 6, by Lorimer et al, reflects specifically on the impact that the pandemic has had on social work students.

VARK: A Guide to Learning Styles. [online] Available at: www.vark-learn.com. This website provides access to the VARK materials.

Williams, S and Rutter, L (2021) *The Practice Educator's Handbook*. London: Sage. Chapter 3 explores effective planning and preparation.

Chapter aims

» To consider the key concepts underpinning student learning including adult learning, experiential learning and the learning environment.

» To explore different teaching strategies and activities that the practice educator can use to develop the student's knowledge and skills.

Critical **questions**

» How does an understanding of learning models enhance your practice?

» How will you structure the student's learning and development on placement?

» What teaching strategies and activities can you use to collaboratively work with the student to develop their knowledge, skills and values?

Introduction

The pivotal role of the practice educator in ensuring effective practice placements, as educators of social work students and as enablers and facilitators of student learning on placement, is outlined in the Practice Educator Professional Standards for social work (PEPS) (BASW, 2022). The PEPS Domain B in particular notes the role of the practice educator in supporting learning and professional development in practice, through awareness of adult learning models, learning needs and the co-ordination of learning opportunities, along with direct teaching.

This chapter will refer briefly to some of the key concepts and ideas underpinning learning: the principles of adult learning, learning models, the impact of the learning environment and the recognition of learning styles. The chapter then considers how this applies to practice educating social work students, including styles of teaching, supporting students from a Black and global minority heritage, supporting students with additional learning needs and giving feedback. Finally, examples of practice education learning activities that can be undertaken with the student are provided.

It should be noted that while this chapter focuses on meeting the student's learning needs, the needs of the service user and the service provider should not be forgotten (Dix, 2018), as will be discussed in Chapter 5. Finally, on assessment, while the Professional Capabilities Framework (PCF) (BASW, 2018) is the primary assessment criteria for social work students in England, local assessment criteria should also be confirmed with both the student and the education provider.

Key concepts underpinning learning

This section considers a number of key concepts that underpin learning, particularly learning within the social work placement. It will consider adult learning, the conscious competence learning model, the learning environment and learning styles. Consideration of these key concepts will contribute to the practice educator's understanding and achievement of PEPS Domains A and B. It may be helpful to read Chapter 4 alongside this section as it explores how knowledge and skills can be developed through experiential learning, reflective practice and critical reflection.

Adult learning

Knowles (1973) refers to the concept of '*andragogy*' and in the original and subsequent editions of the seminal text *The Adult Learner*, common principles are introduced about the ways in which adults learn. While acknowledging andragogical principles originally applied to people aged over 21 years old and some social work students on placement are not yet 21, for the purpose of this discussion social work students on placement are considered to be adult learners. Knowles argues that adults learn best when:

» they know what, why and how they are learning, as learning is enhanced when learners can see the relevance of a learning activity;

» their self-concept is that of being an independent learner and they wish to demonstrate that they are capable of self-directed learning;

» their pre-existing knowledge, experiences and strengths are recognised, used and built upon;

» they are ready to learn, meaning not only that their pre-placement social work education has prepared them for the placement, but also that they attend the placement willing and ready to engage with the learning on placement;

» their learning is goal-orientated, problem-centred and placed in the context of wider goals;

» they are motivated to learn, be that for personal or professional reward, and physical or emotional reward.

(adapted from Knowles et al, 2020, pp 43–7)

These principles can help practice educators understand social work student learning on placement. Students will feel valued and engaged if learning on placement is determined using a collaborative approach; they will have ownership of their own learning and therefore be committed to it, and they will be motivated by feedback that supports the placement goal of meeting the assessment criteria.

However, it is still important not to make any assumptions about the student based on these principles. As a practice educator, you will need to get to know your student in order to find out about their learning needs and uncover their individual motivations. The student may come to a placement with a list of their learning needs and sometimes these can be very broad (*'improve my communication skills'*) or can be a list of things the student wants to do on placement (*'gain experience of report writing'* or *'carry out assessments'*) or simply a list of meeting each of the PCF domains (BASW, 2018). These are often written up before the placement within the placement application form (PAF) and can be generic without the student knowing the specifics of the placement setting.

Student **development exercise**

» As part of the induction activities, ask the student to return to the learning needs listed in their PAF and ask them to review them to ensure that they are placement-specific and sufficiently detailed.

» Ask the student to bring the reviewed list to supervision in order to facilitate a reflective discussion to collaboratively develop a clear understanding of how these learning needs can be met on placement.

This discussion will require the student to reflect on what learning they want to achieve within the placement at both a personal and professional level. By doing this, the practice educator is able to utilise the andragogical principles of relevance, self-concept and respecting previous experience so that the student is now ready, orientated and motivated to learn within the placement. In addition, the task enables the practice educator to develop the supervisory relationship and their understanding of the student to ensure that learning is student-centred.

Social work students may come to their placement motivated by extrinsic factors; for example, to gain a professional qualification for entry into the social work profession and to embark on a new career. However, intrinsic factors also provide motivations for learning; for example, openness to learning and development; being excited by new ideas and ways of working; and seeing the opportunities that the placement offers may also be the impetus for meaningful and deep learning and sustained motivation for personal and professional development.

Conscious competence learning model

One of the roles of the practice educator is to undertake a formative assessment of the student's knowledge and skills and adjust their input to reflect the student's strengths and areas for development. Students can feel consciously competent (*I am good at...*) about some aspects of the placement, while feeling consciously incompetent about others (*I am not confident about...*). However, on occasion the practice educator may notice that the student does not know that they need to develop a skill (unconscious incompetence). Attributed to Burch (1970), the conscious competence learning model is illustrated in Figure 3.1.

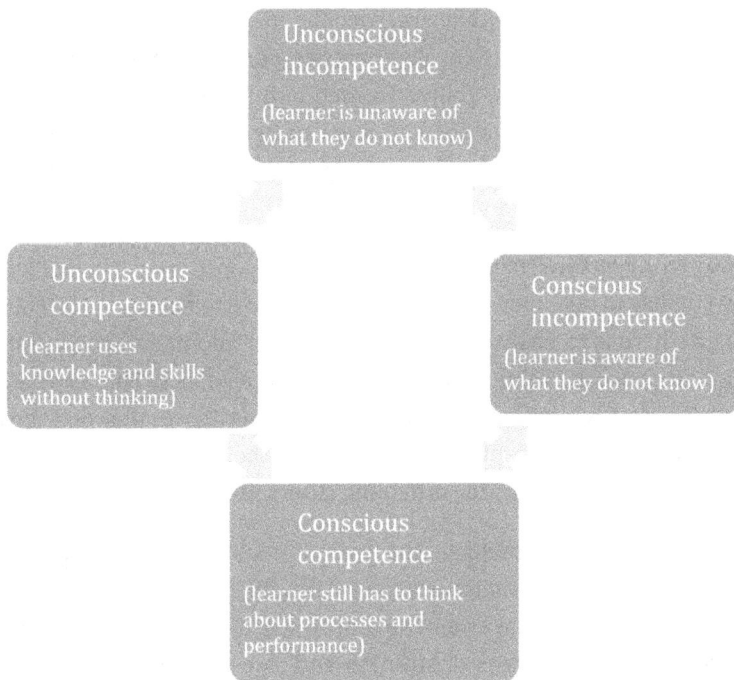

Figure 3.1 The conscious competence learning model (Burch, 1970)

The role of the practice educator is to help the student reach the stage of '*conscious competence*' in a range of knowledge and skills relevant to the placement setting and the PCF (BASW, 2018) assessment criteria. The practice educator's role varies depending on the student's stage of development of the particular knowledge or skill. This can mean the following.

At the *unconscious incompetence* stage, the practice educator needs to focus on helping the student become aware of and acknowledge their learning needs and areas for development. This can be through providing evidence-based feedback that highlights practice. At this stage, it is crucial that the practice educator engages the student tactfully and assertively and ensures that the student is prepared for the impact of hearing for the first time that they have an area for development. It is also important to remember that the student needs to be open to learning from the feedback as when they are feeling overwhelmed by placement, it is not unusual for them to simply *hear*, rather than learn from, the feedback and remain unconsciously incompetent.

At the *conscious incompetence* stage, the student is aware of their areas for development and the practice educator needs to ensure they break down activities and learning into manageable segments. Indeed, the use of the SMART goals model (Doran, 1981) – setting goals that are specific, measurable, achievable, realistic and timely – can be very effective. The practice educator may need to *teach* the student to ensure that they are fully informed and have a good understanding of expectations. The practice educator will need to be reassuring and supportive at this stage, helping the student define, develop and refine their knowledge, skills and understanding.

At the *conscious competence* stage, the student has developed the particular knowledge or skill, but still has to take time to ensure that it is undertaken correctly. The practice educator's role here is to ensure that the student's development, good practice and developing confidence are reinforced through regular feedback. This feedback should include both positive reinforcement and constructive criticism that provides a focus on continuing areas for development. At this stage, the discussion will be more student led, with the practice educator providing stimulation for further development.

At the *unconscious competence* stage, the student is able to practise the knowledge and skill effectively, and the practice educator will help the student focus on analysing their knowledge and learning in order to enable them *'to show their working out'*, both as a method of confirming areas of strength and also to examine areas for further development. This stage is important in acknowledging that learning for professional development is rarely completed.

Finally, a fifth stage, *reflective competence*, has been suggested by Taylor (2007). This is a helpful reminder that learning requires continual reflection, and that assumptions and knowledge have to be open to challenge.

The learning environment

Learning on placement is firmly rooted in the development of knowledge and skills through experience (Kolb, 1984), as outlined in Chapter 4. While this book mainly focuses on the role of the practice educator in placements, it is worth noting that the influence of the learning culture of the organisation and the team, and the learning environment they offer, may promote or hinder student progress. Lave and Wenger (1991) reflect on the importance of a *community of practice* and Chapter 2 of this book, in which we considered preparation, planning and induction, invited you to consider the learning environment and how your team might be experienced by a student. The practice educator can influence and create a positive learning environment by promoting and seeking the active involvement of others in the student's learning so that the student is able to observe a breadth of intervention styles.

We turn now to the facilitation of a conducive learning environment by the practice educator themselves. Firstly, simply ensuring that the student is located within the team room (when office based), and that where possible the practice educator is present on the days that the student is in the office, shows that they value the student and demonstrates that they are invested in their placement and development.

Impact of the pandemic

The learning environment can be significantly impacted when the student is often working and learning from home in a blended placement. The ability for the student to ask informal questions can be restricted, as having to initiate a Teams or phone call for a quick response to a question seems much more daunting than when face to face and may be off-putting. Similarly, the community of practice (Lave and Wenger, 1991) is less available to the student, as other members of the team are also working at home and there is less opportunity to develop working relationships, thus making the preparation points discussed in Chapter 2 more critical.

It is argued that a collaborative approach between practice educator and student values and engages the student, as well as enhancing the student's development of their knowledge and skills (Brodie and Williams, 2013; Beesley, 2022). The notion of collaboration is strengthened by an acknowledgement that learning on placement is a shared enterprise: it is not simply a case of the practice educator *teaching* the student and providing the learning opportunities, as the student is expected to take responsibility for managing their learning and to respond to the opportunities provided. This is highlighted in the Social Work Professional Standards (SWE, 2020), which require all social workers to take responsibility for their own continued professional development. Furthermore, the PCF Domain 1 – Professionalism (BASW, 2018) – requires that a student demonstrates a commitment to continuous learning and development.

Nevertheless, the practice educator bears the initial responsibility for facilitating a collaborative learning environment, which can be achieved by ensuring that the student's opinions and thoughts are always sought first and supplemented by the practice educator to enhance student understanding. The key here is to facilitate the student's learning by ensuring that they are at the centre of their own learning, and that it remains relevant for them within the wider context of passing the placement and becoming a proficient social worker. In other words, it is important that the practice educator ensures that they practise from a student-centred perspective.

However, a final word of warning comes when considering barriers to learning. The practice educator should be aware of the impact of the student's prior experiences of learning, experiences of oppression and lack – or abundance of – self-confidence and self-belief, all of which can act as a potential barrier to the student engaging with the learning activities, as will be discussed in more detail in Chapter 7.

The role of learning styles

Learners are thought to have a preferred or habitual learning style, which informs why they learn best in a certain way. One of the most well-known models of identifying and characterising learning styles is that offered by Honey and Mumford (1992), who identify four different types of learners: Reflectors, Theorists, Activists and Pragmatists.

> **Reflectors:** like to think about an intervention before it occurs, and consider different outcomes and responses to those outcomes. However, they will also spend time after an intervention thinking about how it went and how they could enhance their practice. Planning and reflective discussion are key elements of the reflector's learning style. However, a pitfall can be that they are too busy reflecting on their potential practice to have time to undertake the intervention, so the practice educator may need to impress time limits.

> **Theorists:** like to consider the why of a situation before and/or after it occurs. They like to explore interrelationships between ideas and interventions and will be happy to read up on theories to inform their practice. Intellectual discussion is a key element of the theorist's learning. However, they may

find it difficult to reflect empathically on an intervention, so the practice educator may need to refocus on this area.

Activists: like to learn from doing, particularly from new experiences and problem-solving activities. The use of learning activities within supervision engages the student's learning style, and they will learn through the social worker role itself. However, they may find it difficult to complete learning tasks, particularly the learning from the task, so the practice educator may need to enforce reflective discussion.

Pragmatists: like to see a clear and relevant link between the learning activity and their development. They value constructive feedback and task-centred learning and are often quite structured in their learning. However, they may be reluctant to try new learning opportunities if they do not have sufficient notice, so the practice educator may consider the possibility of duty work to develop their responses to crises.

Learning styles can be helpful to use with students as they can assist the student in developing an awareness of their approaches to learning and identify areas which they need to develop and strengthen; they can also help the practice educator consider the most effective way to suggest a learning task to the student. While it is helpful to understand the student's preferred learning style, it is also important not to become so focused on it that their learning becomes detrimentally affected. The best solution is where all four learning styles are incorporated into the practice educator's repertoire. Indeed, most learners have elements of all learning styles, and it is recognised that different styles and activities keep the student engaged.

Professional **development prompt**

» Reflect on how you prefer to learn. Which of the learning styles do you most identify with?

» With this in mind, how could you support a student whose learning style is, in turn, a reflector, theorist, activist or pragmatist?

As a practice educator, an awareness of your own learning style and how you prefer to learn is essential for your role as an enabler of others; indeed, you and the student may not have the same preferences for learning, which may be a challenge for you. This will involve challenging your own assumptions about how you learn/teach, as well as considering how you will provide varied learning experiences to the student.

Practice educating

It is not unusual that practitioners attending a practice education course feel worried about the *teaching* expectations embedded in the practice educator role and feel that they do not know how to teach or that they have the skills to do so. However, the word teach can be a misnomer, and instead the emphasis here is on the word *educate*. Indeed, the PEPS (BASW, 2022) Domain B requires *'teaching, facilitating and supporting learning and professional development in practice'*, and the subdomains go on to indicate the breadth, flexibility and creativity involved in practice educating a student. For the practice educator, this would mean ensuring that a range of learning tasks and opportunities have been provided that have taken account of the underlying principles of adult learning outlined at the beginning of this chapter, but also that the student is given the opportunity for critical reflection and rigorous analysis of their practice and values, as well as encouraged to consider new and exploratory approaches.

The task of relating theory to practice is a social work education requirement but is often one feared by students and practice educators alike. The practice educator's role is to help students apply their own knowledge, skills and values to practice and to consider how and why a particular theory, method, model or approach has been used; to justify its use and relevance; and to evaluate how effective it has been.

Impact **of the pandemic**

The key concepts remain the same in a blended placement: social work students are still andragogical adult learners (Knowles, 1973) and need to reflect on their strengths and areas for development collaboratively with the practice educator; learning styles (Honey and Mumford, 1992) remain relevant; and experiential learning (Kolb, 1984) remains the predominant focus of learning on placement. The student development activities suggested throughout this book can still be undertaken through remote communication.

Styles of teaching

This section considers how the practice educator can facilitate and promote student learning within the social work placement to enable the development of knowledge and skills. It includes examples of different styles of teaching and providing feedback, supporting students from a Black and global minority heritage and students with additional needs.

A useful way to begin thinking about the teaching element of the practice educator role is first to consider what we mean by teaching and how it is carried out. Jarvis and Gibson (1997) describe three different approaches and styles of teaching within nursing and social work as follows: didactic, Socratic and facilitative.

The *didactic* approach assumes that teachers have knowledge to impart and that they adopt a style of sharing their knowledge. Students are thus *'empty vessels'* to be filled with the teacher's knowledge and are passive recipients of the teacher's knowledge. The teacher is at the centre of this model.

The *Socratic* approach assumes that students are active thinkers, and that the teacher's style is thus more questioning, requiring the student to problem-solve and reflect, with an emphasis on drawing out knowledge from the student, rather than simply putting in the teacher's knowledge.

In the *facilitative* approach, the teacher ensures the conditions and resources for learning are in place and acts as a resource, guide and adviser to the student in the learning process. The student is at the centre of this model.

These three differing approaches can be incorporated by the practice educator at different times in the placement and for different purposes. They can accommodate differing student learning styles, agency and service user needs, or variations in the complexity of the task or at different stages of the task. So, for example, a practice educator may be using a more didactic approach when providing information and initially explaining a particular policy, a new piece of legislation or a particular underpinning theory to a student. However, this would not be enough to ensure learning and the practice educator may later use a more Socratic, questioning, approach, encouraging the student to critically reflect on the implementation of their learning or the particular policy or piece of legislation; for example, how it affects people with lived experience, what particular knowledge and skills they are using in working with service users within the guidelines of the policy and so on. Towards the end of the placement, the practice educator should be able to adopt a facilitative role, where the student is empowered to take the lead in their own learning. The practice educator offers guidance and advice regarding the work and the student's learning, as well as suggesting reading or resources that might help both their work with the service user and their own development.

Supporting students from a Black and global minority heritage

Embarking on a career in social work is not an easy choice for anyone in England at the present time, with the cost of university fees and the cost of living crisis increasingly placing demands on students to work part time alongside their studies, combined with academic expectations to ensure progression, professional requirements to work within, and the inherent pressures of a profession impacted by years of financial reduction and neglect. However, students from a Black and global minority heritage face additional pressures in the face of endemic oppression. Firstly, students from a Black and global minority heritage are more likely to have experienced living in poverty, poor housing, increased health issues and education within an area of economic deprivation, in addition to societal oppression, all of which can have a detrimental impact on student emotional and physical well-being. It is also important to keep in mind that students from a Black and global minority heritage may have experienced other forms of oppression, for example, on grounds of gender, sexuality, disability or faith, which compound their experiences of racism. Crenshaw (1989) introduced the concept of intersectionality, initially to ensure that women from a Black and global minority heritage who experience both sexism and racism were '*seen*'; however, this initial definition has now been extended to incorporate any form of multi-faceted oppression. These factors should be taken into account when supporting a student from a Black and global minority heritage on placement and the practice educator's role here is to acknowledge the experience of oppression and to value the student's self-identified identity throughout their work and in particular within the supervisory relationship (McCaughan et al, 2018).

In addition, there has been an identified increase in the number of students from a Black and global minority heritage who fail their placement, resulting in additional costs and time before they are able to enter paid employment and earn a wage as a qualified worker (Fairtlough et al, 2014). However, it is important to note that learning experiences for students from a Black and global minority heritage, even where they pass their placement, require attention in terms of practice educator awareness and skills (Caffrey and Fruin, 2019). Indeed, Tedam (2014) found that students from a Black and global minority heritage experienced over-scrutiny and lower expectations in relation to the development of their knowledge and skills, combined with a lack of support from the practice educator. It is therefore clear that practice educators need to be aware of the impact of this on their student and to reflect on their practice and assumptions to ensure that they are supporting and assessing students from a Black and global minority heritage appropriately and fairly.

Professional **development prompt**

Your student, Rimna, who is of Pakistani heritage, tells you that her mother has returned to Pakistan for a month and left her responsible for the younger children, housework and cleaning. She is sorry that she has arrived at the placement late each day this week and tells you that she has now arranged for them to be walked to and from school by a neighbour. However, she wants to discuss with you leaving at four o'clock each day to support the family.

» How do you respond?

This is an ethical dilemma as, although supporting Rimna to be able to support her family is very important and may appear to be a short-term issue, she will miss five hours per week of placement and finishing early can often reduce learning opportunities that can only be undertaken at that point in the day. You could negotiate a half-hour lunch break to reduce the impact of the hours lost and be clear with her that it is a short-term agreement. You could discuss with her the option of working from home some days to reduce travel time but, as discussed in Chapter 2, distance working still requires availability. Furthermore, it would be worth considering if there were any school holidays in the period and discussing the possibility of Rimna taking time off from the placement if this were the case. Finally, a discussion with Rimna about her responsibilities at home will be invaluable to explore if there are other people around to support her or short-term solutions that could reduce the need to undertake household chores. The point of this activity is to start you thinking about different cultural responsibilities and roles that might be given to the student and how you will respond to them. It is important that you are non-judgemental and supportive, yet remain aware of the demands of placement learning and, ultimately, assessment.

As has been discussed above, the learning environment can be enhanced through a collaborative and student-centred approach by the practice educator. This comes from understanding the student so that a responsive approach can be taken that meets the student's individual learning needs (Beesley, 2022). The MANDELA model (Tedam, 2012), which is outlined in Chapter 4, may be helpful for practice educators in developing an understanding of their student.

Supporting students with a disability

The Office for Students (OfS) (2021) reported that the number of students with a disability in higher education rose significantly between 2010 and 2020, with

14.3 per cent of full-time students now self-identifying as having a disability. However, as this was based on self-report at the start of the academic course, it may be that this statistic is not truly representative of students with a disability within higher education. This number includes students with a learning disability, such as dyslexia or dyspraxia, a mental health condition, a sensory or physical disability and a social or communication impairment (OfS, 2021). Disability is a protected characteristic under the Equality Act 2010, and placement providers have a duty to meet these needs where possible.

Students with a disability can apply for a Reasonable Adjustment Plan (RAP), which summarises the impact of the student's disability on their ability to access learning. This is primarily focused on academic teaching and assessment, but good practice dictates that placement learning requirements should also be included. While this cannot be shared with the practice educator without the student's consent, if a student chooses not to declare a disability to the practice educator, they cannot later state that they were not afforded reasonable adjustment. However, Hunt and Mathews (2018) reflect that sometimes students choose not to disclose their disability due to a fear of discrimination or rejection from the placement, so it is good to revisit with the student in induction if they have any reasonable adjustments that they have not yet shared.

The practice educator should familiarise themself with the student's declared disability, both through discussion with the student and listening to the impact that this has on them as an individual, and through reading existing guidance. In addition, there may be physical adjustments that need to be made to facilitate the student's learning, for example, specialist IT equipment, a particular type of chair or desk, or the provision of accessible parking. Remember that completion of these tasks may take some time, and that it is your responsibility to ensure that the necessary preparation for placement, as discussed in Chapter 2, is completed.

The social model of disability (Oliver, 1990) states that it is society's norms, beliefs and oppressive practices that impair the student, rather than their disability. It is therefore incumbent on the practice educator to provide a learning environment that facilitates the student's ability to engage with learning opportunities, rather than to expect the student to conform to placement setting norms. Placement can have a higher emotional toil for students with a disability because they find the workplace more tiring than others, possibly because of the extreme mental effort required to conform to societal expectations; they may have low self-esteem and lack confidence in their abilities; and they may feel isolated and think that other students are learning procedures and tasks far more quickly than they are. However, it is important to note that students with a disability often have a variety of strengths which they have developed throughout their personal, educational and professional experiences.

During the placement period, the practice educator is responsible for ensuring that each individual student is able to access learning opportunities, and we will now look at specific disabilities, including learning disabilities, autism and physical disabilities. Considering first students with dyslexia and dyspraxia, Hewson and Gant (2020) identified that there needs to be greater understanding of learning disabilities, of how they affect students on placement and acceptance of them as commonplace disabilities. Dyslexia, for example, can come in many forms and impact not just reading and writing, but also memory and processing information, number recognition, organisational skills, following instructions, remembering names and sense of direction, while dyspraxia can impact fine motor skills such as handwriting.

Students with dyslexia are likely to find completing placement tasks more difficult; the practice educator has an important role in allocating additional administrative time and supporting the student to develop effective coping strategies to enable them to meet deadlines. Strategies for practice educators to support students with dyslexia include the following.

Induction:

» give lots of opportunities for observation of practice;

» demonstrate and explain procedures simply;

» provide the student with a placement pack, setting out useful information and standard procedures for them to refer back to;

» with the student, draw up a plan for the placement at the beginning, highlighting important information and dates.

Planning:

» set clear, measurable learning outcomes;

» ask the student to repeat/outline what they are going to do;

» do not give too many instructions at once, particularly if the instructions are only given verbally;

» give instructions in both written and verbal form wherever possible;

» explain tasks more than once.

Supervision:

» provide materials in advance of their necessity to enable the student to prepare;

» consider more frequent but shorter supervision sessions, as processing information may take longer or too much information may be overwhelming for the student;

» provide additional time in structured supervisory sessions to go through administrative procedures and routines for placement;

» encourage reflection;

» record the discussion so that they can concentrate on the discussion rather than taking notes and can access the discussion again afterwards.

Reading:

» allow extra time for reading;

» provide a quiet space/room for the student to read in;

» present the student with reading well in advance of meetings, highlighting important parts if appropriate;

» provide opportunities to discuss reading;

» allow students to print documents using larger print or coloured paper, as per their RAP.

Writing:

» provide exemplar reports so the student has a clear idea about the level and content required and the expected format;

» discuss with the student the main points that should be covered prior to writing the document;

» allow extra time for students to write reports and other paperwork – encourage them to diarise this time on a regular basis;

» proofread and provide constructive feedback;

» where possible, allow the student to submit draft reports with a font they find easy to use.

When considering social work students with autism, be aware that starting placement is likely to be overwhelming for the student, as new environments are challenging. The practice educator should facilitate the development of a routine to support the individual needs of the student. Furthermore, the student may need regular breaks, as social interaction can be exhausting for a student with autism. While autism is traditionally associated, and one can say stereotyped, with limited communication, it is important to remember that high-functioning autistic students may mask their autistic traits well.

It is important to note that there will be social work students with physical disabilities, including those with mobility, visual or hearing impairment. While their physical needs should have been addressed before they started the placement, it is important to continue to support their learning needs within the placement. Thought may need to be given to which service users the student can and cannot support; for example, allocating them a service user who lives on the third floor of a building without a lift is not accessible for a student who has mobility issues. The issue of communication may need to be addressed; for example, if the student requires a sign language interpreter or sighted support worker, ensure that they have also met the placement's Disclosure and Barring Service (DBS) requirements and understand the issues of confidentiality within a social work placement.

The number of students in full-time higher education who are experiencing issues with their mental health has increased over the last decade (OfS, 2021). This ranges from where the student can usually manage their placement well with flexibility and understanding from the practice educator to periods where the placement needs to be suspended. In most cases, the student is emotionally intelligent and aware of their own mental health, their triggers and warning signs, as well as being cognisant of their coping strategies and limitations. In such cases, discussions in induction and supervision can enhance the practice educator's understanding, as can reading around the subject. However, it is important that the student receives non-judgemental and understanding responses from the practice educator, as the stigma attached to mental health often deters students from sharing details (Kotera et al, 2018).

In conclusion, students may have a range of different disabilities, and those discussed here are certainly not exhaustive. However, an essential aspect of the practice educator role is a discussion with the student to determine how it impacts them and what support they would like, combined with a non-judgemental response that accepts the student for who they are and supports them as required. This collaborative approach to practice education is critical to reduce the power differential and engage the student.

Giving feedback

An important part of facilitating learning is the provision of feedback. This can be on the practice carried out by the student, their approach, their values and their overall progress, as well as the explicit feedback that is required after a direct observation (and which is referred to in more detail in Chapter 6 on assessment). The guidance on feedback offered in this chapter recognises the crucial place that feedback can play in teaching, inspiring and developing confidence, as well as improving student emotional intelligence, performance and understanding. Positive feedback is important as it tells the student what they are doing well, boosts confidence and engages the andragogical principle of learning for intrinsic reward. However, when providing positive feedback, it is helpful to include some challenge for the student for continuing learning to build upon their strengths. In comparison, constructive feedback involves raising an area for development. Nevertheless,

feedback is defined as a process through which learners make sense of information from various sources and use it to enhance their work or learning strategies. This definition goes beyond notions that feedback is principally about teachers informing students about strengths, weaknesses and how to improve, and highlights the centrality of the student role in sense-making and using comments to improve subsequent work.

(Carless and Boud, 2018, p 1315)

The way in which the practice educator manages the feedback process is one strategy to facilitate and encourage student learning. An excellent way to start the feedback discussion is first asking the student how they feel, which enables the practice educator to assess the student's understanding and deliver the feedback appropriately. A number of feedback models will now be presented.

Firstly, the feedback sandwich must be mentioned. Although it has lost popularity in recent years, the premise is that the practice educator offers positive feedback sandwiched before and after constructive feedback. The acknowledgement of the student's strengths enables them to accept the practice educator's identification of their weakness (Carless and Boud, 2018). Furthermore, the student is left hearing a positive about their practice, and so is motivated to address the area for development to gain further positive feedback. However, as the student can be conditioned to wait for the constructive feedback, the effectiveness of the positive feedback may be lost. Nevertheless, the principle that constructive feedback should include positives remains.

A commonly used and helpful feedback model is the use of the acronym SCORE, which stands for Specific, Clear, Owned, Relevant, Enabling.

Specific: it is important that feedback is evidence based and about a particular element of learning or behaviour, for example '*it was good when you said...*' or '*in the visit with Miss X I noticed that you seemed overwhelmed when...*'. The first element of accessing feedback is the understanding of what the area for development is. If the student does not understand what is expected of them then they will be unable to address it.

Clear: the feedback should be accessible for the student. Ensure that feedback is clear and understandable. It is better to make one or two points which are more likely to be remembered, as multiple points can be overwhelming and unlikely to be remembered or engaged with. The STAR model can be used to help clarity:

Situation or Task: outline the situation or task that is referred to;

Action: outline the student's actions within the incident;

Result: outline the consequence of the behaviour.

Owned: feedback should start with '*I have noticed that...*' or a similar phrase, so that the student can see that the practice educator is engaged in the process and values them as learners. Where feedback is second hand from a colleague, it can be helpful to ask the colleague to attend a proportion of the discussion or write up their feedback to work from. Where it is the practice educator's opinion, they should ensure that they are clear that this is the case, '*it seemed to me ...*', so that the student understands the basis for their statement.

Relevant: give feedback as soon as possible; feedback over 24 hours after the event immediately loses relevancy and impact. Furthermore, ensure that the feedback is relevant to the student, their practice and their assessment criteria; for example, is feedback on their navigation skills important? It could be considered appropriate if they are constantly late for appointments and it is impacting their professionalism, but not if it does not impact the service user.

Enabling: prepare for the feedback, choose an appropriate time and location and ensure privacy. Think about the language being used and approach the feedback as a constructive dialogue. Ensure that the feedback is solution focused, with a clear plan of potential support for the student to access, reminding them that the practice educator is there to support and not criticise.

A further way to consider providing feedback is the use of restorative practice, where the practice educator provides both high support and high challenge to maximise student engagement. The restorative matrix in Figure 3.2 regarding the balance of support/challenge is adapted from Wachtel and McCold's (2001) original matrix.

High support/ low challenge	High support/ high challenge
'That was great.'	*'I really liked the way you encouraged Miss C to respond and listen so well.... I wondered if she understood some of the terminology that you used?'*

Low support/low challenge	Low support/high challenge
'That was okay, bits of it could've been better.'	*'What did you say that for? Why didn't you explain it properly?'*

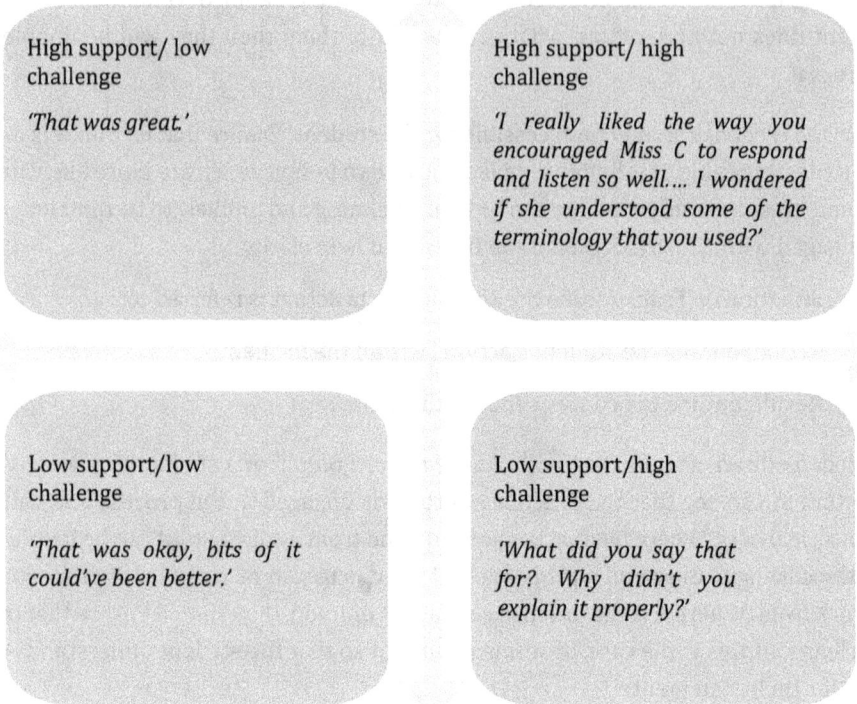

Figure 3.2 Restorative feedback. Adapted from Wachtel and McCold (2001)

It can be seen that with both low-challenge approaches, the student is left with nothing to develop, as there are no specifics on what needs to be addressed. In contrast, with both of the low-support approaches, the student is left deflated and their confidence undermined. However, with the high-support/high-challenge approach the practice educator provides constructive feedback and supports students to address the areas for development, so the student feels clear on both the issues to address and how they can do this.

Professional **development prompt**

» Think about a time when you have received feedback about an aspect of your practice.

» Consider what made the feedback helpful or unhelpful.

» Did the feedback offer you high support and high challenge? If not, how could the feedback to you have been improved?

Where you have experienced feedback that you found productive, it is helpful to consider what it was that made it productive so that you recreate that strategy for giving feedback to the student. Equally, however, if you have experienced feedback that was not productive or, worse, counter-productive or destructive, you can still reflect on practice that you would not wish to replicate.

Be aware that giving and receiving feedback is not always easy and can provoke strong feelings of anxiety on both sides. The student may not have developed resilience to hearing constructive feedback or may have developed poor coping strategies such as anger, silence or denial and blaming; it is the practice educator's role to develop the skill of accepting feedback (Carless and Boud, 2018), as they would any other skill.

Student **development exercise**

> » In induction, ask the student how they react to feedback and if there is any way that you as the practice educator can give it that will engage them to hear and access feedback more productively.

Furthermore, students may be anxious about failing their placement, which may be exacerbated by the pressure of increased student fees or family expectations that can prevent a student from accessing feedback. It is important here to reassure the student that feedback is intended to provide the opportunity to work collaboratively to enhance their practice rather than functioning as a punitive measure. By having solutions to offer, this can reassure the student that this is the case.

However, it is important to note that equally sometimes the practice educator can shy away from giving challenging feedback, as they may be anxious about an adverse reaction or hurting the student's feelings. Finch (2017) reminds us of the importance of courageous conversations as without feedback the unconsciously incompetent (Burch, 1970) student cannot begin to address their areas for development, and therefore stagnates and fails to develop their knowledge and skills.

Finally, it follows that the practice educator should also be open to receiving feedback about their role from their student, mentor and colleagues, viewing this as helpful information for their developing role as a practice educator and thus meeting Domain D of the PEPS (BASW, 2022) requirements.

Practice education learning activities

The practice educator's role is to facilitate learning through the provision of appropriate learning opportunities for the student. This will primarily involve appropriate caseload allocations that ensure a breadth of workload that reflects all aspects of the placement agency. A further role of the practice educator is the modelling of good practice, often through co-working, which should also be supplemented by arranging for the student to observe and co-work with colleagues to provide a variety of intervention styles. Other learning activities include:

» role play of a specific task or skill;

» suggested reading on a topic to aid student theoretical understanding followed by discussion in supervision;

» reflective questions during supervision to help the student to explore and clarify theories or models underpinning their practice;

» specifically focused activities within supervision to support the development of an assessed learning need;

» reading, discussing student written pieces of work or critical reflections;

» reading, discussing student case recording, assessments and any work-related products;

» project work – such as developing an agency resource pack or working with a particular group of people with lived experience.

Throughout this book, *student development exercises* are provided for the practice educator to use with the student. This section now illustrates two different learning activities: the knowledge, values, skills, theories grid and the Theory Circle.

Knowledge, values, skills, theories grid

A simple exercise is the knowledge, values, skills, theories grid (Figure 3.3) for unpicking underpinning elements of practice.

Student **development exercise**

» Ask the student to reflect on one piece of work undertaken between supervisions, considering how each of the four elements has been addressed. The grid can then be used as a base for reflective discussion during supervision, with the student taking the lead and the practice educator developing the discussion through the use of open questions and sharing practice wisdom.

Knowledge	Theories
Values	Skills

Figure 3.3 Knowledge, values, skills, theories grid

The preparation before supervision by the student affords the student time to contemplate the different areas and prepare for reflective discussion within social work student supervision. However, it also enables the practice educator to gauge the student's understanding of the intervention, which facilitates a student-led level of support to be offered that meets their learning needs. Indeed, when considering Vygotsky's (1978) Zone of Peripheral Development, by understanding the student's existing strengths and areas for development the practice educator can push the student a little further than they are currently able to comfortably go while understanding the developmental boundaries.

Finally, the grid can also help students when preparing written practice-related case studies for inclusion in their portfolio, if required.

The Theory Circle

The use of a particular visual framework for helping the student identify the theories they are using to inform their practice can be very helpful. An example of this is the Theory Circle (Collingwood, 2005). This is a three-stage process that is used with the student as follows.

Stage 1: KIT

Prepare the profile 'KIT', as illustrated in Figure 3.4. Begin by drawing a stick person and then begin to make a very basic profile (using keywords) which identifies the person. This can include the following: age, gender, race, culture, history, family, friends, likes, dislikes, life events, significant other agency connections, wants, etc. The profile can be drawn up by the student with the person or used simply as an exercise in itself.

Case **example**

Leszek is a student in a statutory children and families team, who is about halfway through his final placement. He has shown some good social work skills, but you feel that he is an activist learner at the expense of his application of theory to the case. You have allocated a new case to him, and you are collaboratively planning his first visit to the family. Keitha is a ten-year-old girl whose teacher has placed a referral to your team as she has lost weight recently and is described as gaunt. There is a history of maternal alcohol misuse, and you understand that dad left the family home six months ago. There are three younger brothers in the house, who the school have no concerns about, but Keitha may be caring for them on a regular basis.

You ask Leszek to complete Stage 1 of the Theory Circle within supervision. Figure 3.4 is Leszek's completed Stage 1 KIT.

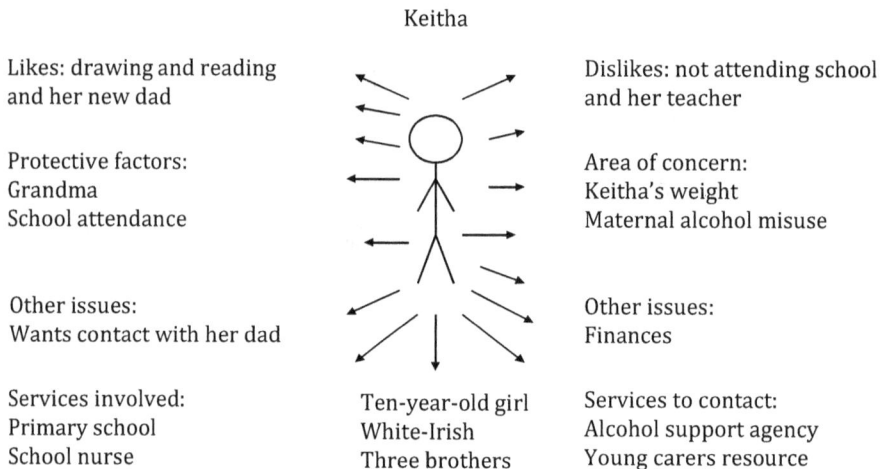

Keitha

Likes: drawing and reading and her new dad		Dislikes: not attending school and her teacher
Protective factors: Grandma School attendance		Area of concern: Keitha's weight Maternal alcohol misuse
Other issues: Wants contact with her dad		Other issues: Finances
Services involved: Primary school School nurse	Ten-year-old girl White-Irish Three brothers	Services to contact: Alcohol support agency Young carers resource

Figure 3.4 Stage 1 KIT

Case **example (continued)**

» What constructive feedback would you give Leszek in relation to his completion of KIT?

» Are there any other areas that you might consider including on KIT?

By undertaking Stage 1, Leszek has demonstrated his understanding of the issues that affect Keitha. He has been able to demonstrate his professionalism and accountability by summarising the case for the practice educator within the KIT. The practice educator should have read the referral and may ask open questions and offer practice wisdom to enhance Leszek's understanding of the referral.

Stage 2: the Theory Circle

The second stage of the Theory Circle requires reflection on two different sorts of theory and knowledge, as illustrated in Figure 3.5. Firstly, the 'theory to inform' looks at theories that may explain the impact of life experiences on the person, which ensures an empathic understanding when first meeting Keitha. A word of warning: just because a life experience may have had an impact does not mean that it has, so it is important to remember not to make an assumption but to listen to the service user's individual perspective. The second element of Stage 2 is the 'theory to inform', which considers the models of intervention that could be used by the social worker when they work with the service user. This can include a variety of models for consideration.

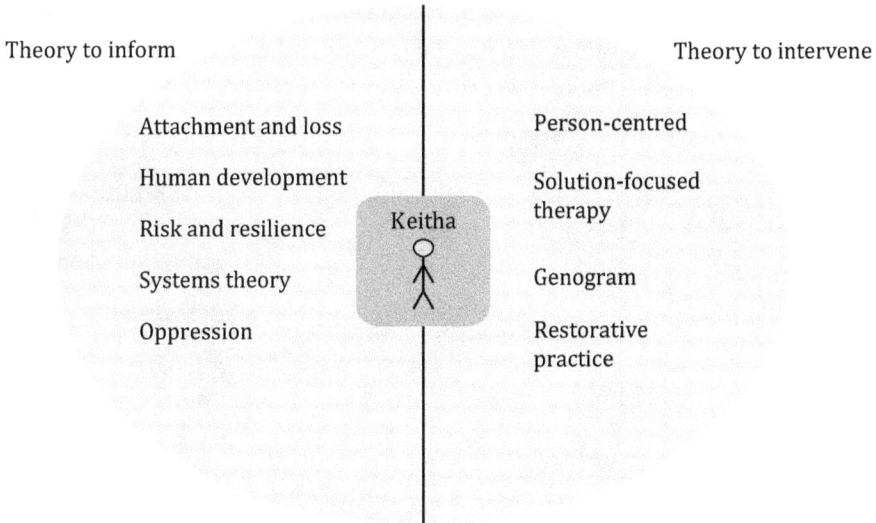

Theory to inform   Theory to intervene

Attachment and loss   Person-centred

Human development   Solution-focused
                                                   therapy
Risk and resilience   Keitha

Systems theory   Genogram

Oppression   Restorative
                                                   practice

Figure 3.5 Stage 2: the Theory Circle

Case **example (continued)**

Leszek has also prepared Stage 2 of the Theory Circle and presents
Figure 3.5 in social work student supervision.

» *How would you explore this with Leszek?*

By undertaking Stage 2 before the intervention, Leszek is planning the intervention in a more holistic way than just when to visit and what to say. Leszek is able to develop an understanding of some of the issues that may impact Keitha, explore his understanding of them and is able to attend the first home visit in a much more informed manner, thus enhancing his ability to engage the family.

Stage 3: knowledge, skills and values

Within Stage 3 the student considers what may inform practice, for example what knowledge, skills and values they may use, as illustrated in Figure 3.6. This builds the student's understanding further as they are asked to reflect on pertinent knowledge that they will need, such as placement setting requirements and the skills they will need. They are given an opportunity to discuss the concepts and theory behind these social work skills, and the values that may be present within the intervention.

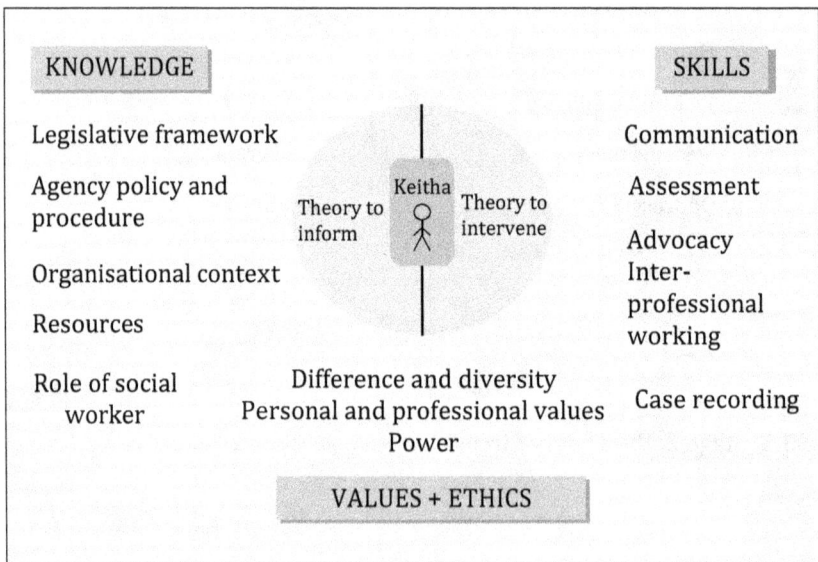

Figure 3.6 Stage 3: knowledge, skills and values

Case **example concludes**

Finally, Leszek has added Stage 3 to the Theory Circle, enabling him to consider the knowledge, skills and values that he may utilise in his home visit to Keitha and her family.

» Please reflect on how you would complete the learning activity with Leszek.

It is clear from this discussion that there are numerous areas to reflect upon and discuss when working with Keitha and her family. It is fair to reflect that the Theory Circle, when undertaken thoroughly with a student, can potentially consume a whole supervision, so may need some strategic planning or an additional supervision session. However, the development of the student's knowledge and skills within the activity can be significant.

Professional **development prompt**

» In light of some of the suggestions given in this chapter about how you might enable students' development of knowledge and skills, and taking into account your own learning style, consider the following:

  » How have you judged the success of your role as an enabler and facilitator of student learning?

  » Which particular teaching/enabling strategies worked for you, and why? Did they also work for the student? Reflect if they would work equally well for another student with different learning needs and style.

  » What have been the highlights of the teaching/facilitating role for you?

  » What have you not felt so comfortable with?

This reflection on your practice education skill will be invaluable in meeting Domain D of the PEPS (BASW, 2022), '*developing knowledge and continuing performance as a practice educator*'. Many qualifying practice education courses will require you to reflect on your development as a practice educator, as you are encouraged to do here.

Conclusion

This chapter has focused on the enabling and teaching elements of the practice educator role and what a practice educator can do to help facilitate student learning on placement. Key concepts underpinning learning have been discussed, and exercises, teaching tools and strategies have been suggested which can help the practice educator in their enabling and teaching role. Further chapters – Chapter 4 on critical reflection and values, Chapter 5 on reflective supervision, and Chapter 6 on assessment – provide further information and guidance on the enabling elements of the practice educator role.

Taking it further

Knowles, M, Holton III, E F, Swanson, R A and Robinson, P A (2020) *The Adult Learner: The Definitive Classic in Adult Education and Human Resource Development*. Abingdon: Routledge. This updated classic by Malcolm Knowles and colleagues provides a robust discussion of andragogical principles.

Maclean, S and Harrison, R (2014) *Social Work Theory: A Straightforward Guide for Practice Educators and Placement Supervisors*. Rugeley: Kirwin Maclean. This comprehensive guide to theory provides an excellent refresher for practice educators who are feeling intimated by the need to talk theory with the student. Alternatively, Maclean's Social Work Theory cards and Reflective Practice cards can be used.

Taplin, S (ed) (2018) *Innovations in Practice Learning*. St Albans: Critical Publishing. This book provides an excellent insight into a range of issues that impact student learning and offers knowledge for the practice educator to apply to their practice education practice.

Chapter 4 | Critical reflection and values

Chapter aims

» To enable practice educators to explore what critical reflection means to them.

» To examine key models designed to develop understanding of social work values.

» To offer practice educators methods to use with students to facilitate development of knowledge and skills in critical reflection and to consider values.

Critical **questions**

» How do you model critically reflective practice for your student in the context of a challenging working environment?

» How do you help a student to develop their own critical reflection?

» How do you ensure that the teaching of values is integrated with other aspects of practice?

Introduction

This chapter will meet the Practice Educator Professional Standards for social work (PEPS) (BASW, 2022) subdomains A3: *'Create reflective spaces for learners' growth and development and provide regular reflective supervision'*; B3 *'Help students to understand their own learning processes and to develop different models and strategies for critical reflection and analysis'*; and D2 *'Show understanding of, and the ability to apply, models and theories of supervision, knowledge and research on assessment, teaching and learning, and critical reflection'*. It is noted that supporting critical reflection on the student's values will in turn enable the practice educator to meet the statement of values.

Practice education involves challenge and complexity. It demands the negotiation and management of interpersonal relationships between the practice educator and student, within wider contexts, environments and regulations that are ever-changing. It requires the practice educator to play the roles of educator, supporter, manager, assessor, enabler, facilitator, supervisor, teacher, negotiator, planner, mediator and probably more in these testing times. The multi-layered and sometimes contested nature of each of these roles means that practice education is and has to be a thinking enterprise. Within each of these roles practice educators will be challenged in their practice and will have to critically reflect upon it. This inevitably encompasses thinking about ethical practice with social work values at the core.

Critical reflection can be described as contemplation on self to enhance knowledge, skills and values; the observation of practice to identify good practice that can be assimilated into your own practice; the development of understanding of other people's behaviours and responses to your practice; and the consideration of the context within which the profession of social work operates. It is an understanding that critical reflection on skill development is underpinned by application of theory and is seen as a holistic activity (Ingram, 2015). Indeed, it is argued that emotionally intelligent social work education enhances reflective practice and the development of knowledge, skills and values (Ingram, 2015). Furthermore Scragg (2019) emphasises the importance of the supervisory relationship in engaging the student in reflective activity.

It can be argued that there are two stages of reflection within social work practice – reflective practice and critical reflection – which will be outlined below. The Professional Capabilities Framework (PCF) (BASW, 2018) has been designed to reflect the interrelatedness of values, diversity, justice, knowledge, skills, contexts and organisations, and it is therefore axiomatic that the student will need to develop skills of analysis in order to make sense of their practice. Finally, where a social worker has reflected and consequently enhanced their practice, there will be improved outcomes for service users (Ferguson, 2018).

Practice educators are guided by the PCF (BASW, 2018), the Social Work Professional Standards (SWE, 2020) and the Code of Ethics for Social Work (BASW, 2021) and, in addition, their role as practice educator is governed by the PEPS Values Statement (BASW, 2022) (as set out in Chapter 1). Any discussion of social work values is complex, and it is not the intent here to provide a thorough exploration of values: instead, we direct the reader to authors such as Banks, Beckett et al, Tedam, and Thompson, all of whom are mentioned in the 'Taking it further' section at the end of this chapter. It is pertinent also to reflect that adherence to social work values necessitates an understanding of ethics, diversity, oppression, human rights and social justice.

This chapter focuses on the development of critical reflection and offers guidance for practice educators in helping students to develop the requisite skills to enable them both to reflect *on action* – including written reflections and collaborative reflective discussion – and to reflect *in action* – including reflective practice in action and decision making. The chapter also considers the student's social work values, where models and exercises in relation to the social GGRRAAACCEEESSS model, PCS model and SHARP framework are presented.

Key concepts underpinning reflection

It is important that the practice educator develops an understanding of the concepts that underpin critical reflection, both to reflect on their own practice and to promote the development of the student's reflective skills. In this section, the concept of the reflective practitioner, reflective practice, social work values and critical reflection are outlined.

Reflective practitioner

The concept of the *reflective practitioner* (Schön, 1983) acknowledges that a practitioner makes reflective decisions in the moment that rely on a combination of their knowledge base, skill set and the needs of the individual situation: Schön called this *'reflection in action'*. It is important to recognise that it is possible for the practitioner to implement evidence-based decision making while in the act of undertaking an intervention. However, Schön identified a second reflective point, where, after the intervention, the practitioner reflects on their work and uses their understanding of what worked successfully to inform future practice, as well as critically analysing how the task could be undertaken in a different way to optimise future outcomes and indeed to enable further reflection in action. He called this *'reflection on action'*.

This distinction is important for the social work student, as it is the reflection on action that is often the practice educator's focus when discussing reflective practice with the aim of developing the student's knowledge and skills. However, the ability to reflect in action is an equally important social work skill (Ferguson, 2018) and this will be discussed towards the end of this chapter.

Reflective practice

Reflective practice is important in the development of professional practice as it enables us to learn from our experiences of working with others. It includes reviewing and analysing an experience, drawing conclusions and learning lessons and incorporating them into future actions. Indeed, it can be seen that reflective practice is aligned with Kolb's (1984) experiential learning cycle, which developed the idea of how to reflect on action. It has subsequently been modified in a variety of ways, but all have the same underpinning principles, which are that adults learn best by doing (Knowles, 1973).

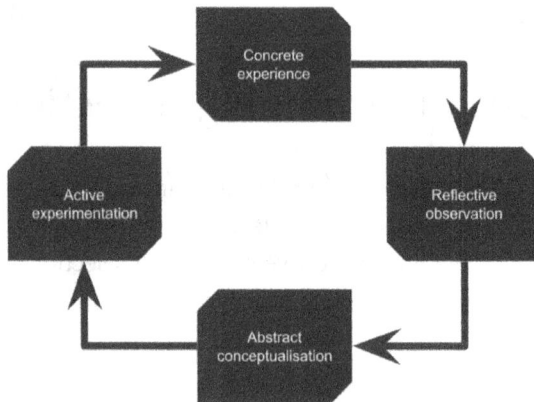

Figure 4.1 Kolb's (1984) experiential learning cycle

As Figure 4.1 shows, the experiential learning cycle requires the person to undertake an activity that provides concrete experience, which they are then asked to reflect upon to consider what they felt went well and what did not go as well as expected. This is followed by a period of abstract conceptualisation, where the person applies theory and knowledge to the situation to develop an understanding of why the result was as it was, and to consider different theories to inform future practice. This is followed by a planning stage, where different options are considered to enable consideration of the most appropriate way to undertake the activity again. The importance of this model lies in its assertion that learning is not simply the acquisition of knowledge as a result of experience, but that it also requires reflection and the application of theory to facilitate understanding and the development of knowledge, skills and values.

Social work student placements are based on experiential learning. Indeed, the development of the practice of reflection is afforded significant emphasis as one of the nine core social work assessment criteria (BASW, 2018). Students can success-fully and independently reflect using the model of experiential learning (Kolb, 1984; Gibbs, 1988), understanding why an incident happened in the way it did and learning from it, using *internal supervision* (Ferguson, 2018). However, it can be argued that independent experiential learning alone is insufficient when developing social work knowledge, skills and values, and that reflective discussion in supervision (Davys and

Beddoe, 2009) enhances learning by the use of open questions and sharing of the practice educator's practice wisdom.

The desired outcome of reflective practice is to work towards the best outcomes for service users, as well as the professional development of social work knowledge, skills and values. However, reflective practice is also beneficial as it enhances accountability and ethical practice because when the student is aware of the impact of self on service users and interventions, they are more likely to practise in an ethical manner. Finally, research has identified that those students who were better able to reflect on their thoughts, feelings and beliefs were more resilient and able to manage stress (Kinman and Grant, 2013).

Developing reflective practice requires a commitment to developing ways of reviewing your own practice so that reflection becomes routine.

Professional **development prompt**

» How can you create a reflective space for the student?

Higgins (2019) recommends the development of a '*reflective space*', that is, considering both a time and a location to enable creative reflection. Social work students are afforded study time, often a day a fortnight, which is designed to enable concentrated time to complete written reflections or research on topics related to the placement. However, where reflection is relegated to a once-fortnightly activity, it does not become habitual. Therefore, supporting the student to plan regular reflective time is as important as scheduling any other routine appointments. The commute to and from the placement can afford time to reflect; however, actively scheduling ten minutes' reflection time after each intervention reinforces the importance of reflective practice to the student.

The PCF End of First Placement (BASW, 2018) requires the student to be able to '*with guidance, use reflection*', thus indicating that, in the first placement, the student is expected, with support, to develop the skills to enable them to be able to engage effectively in reflective practice. Many social work students on placement are already able to reflect competently on their own practice, or that of their colleagues. However, it is not unusual in the first half of the first placement for the student to be stuck in one direction of reflective practice. Where the student focuses purely on colleagues' practice, the practice educator will need to support them to move into self-reflection.

Similarly, where the student's self-reflection is focused entirely on either their own strengths or their areas for development, the practice educator's role is to widen their reflections to consider how they can learn by reflecting on the practice of others.

However, it is important that the student does not just undertake reflective practice, where they identify their strengths and areas for development or identify how an intervention could have been undertaken differently, but also that the student demonstrates the ability to transfer learning from one situation to the next, effectively ensuring that they continue round the experiential learning cycle (Kolb, 1984; Gibbs, 1988), gaining and developing knowledge and skills.

Social work values

Reflective practice should not focus solely on practical skills; it should also incorporate reflection on social work values as the development of the student's professional values is of equal importance. Social work values are the worth that is accorded by the profession to a behaviour or opinion (Beckett et al, 2017), thus governing how social workers should act and think. This may appear to be *'controlling'* in a profession that promotes choice as a core value, but as Beckett et al remind us, it is social work values that enable the profession to make often life-changing ethical decisions and inform good practice. Banks (2021) argues that social work practice centres on engaging in ethical dilemmas, which requires the weighing up of different perspectives in decision making. She argues that ethics are developed from moral norms and moral philosophy. Thus, ethics are socially constructed to reflect the prevailing culture, making the term *'ethical practice'* one that reflects the expectations of the profession. It is important to remember that social work values are subject to review and change and will develop as the profession develops.

Nevertheless, anti-discriminatory and anti-oppressive practice remain the cornerstones of ethical social work practice. Thompson (2021, p 5) argues that discrimination is the *'disadvantage, disempowerment and oppression'* of a person or group of people because of their identity. He argues that the Personal, Cultural, Structural (PCS) analysis model, as discussed below, enables the identification and understanding of discrimination, from a personal, cultural and structural perspective. Tedam (2021) argues that oppression is the unfair use of power and privilege, and that anti-oppressive practice is a way to fight for and promote social justice and human rights. In the later sections of this chapter, student development exercises are provided which can be used by practice educators to enhance the student's reflections on their values, including the social GGRRAAACCEEESSS model, the PCS model and the SHARP framework.

Critical reflection

Critical reflection implies reflective practice that looks beyond the student's strengths and areas for development with an awareness that social work practice does not exist in isolation, but that any intervention is affected by societal factors, which should be considered and analysed to give the student a deeper understanding of the situation or intervention. Indeed, deep learning (Marton and Saljo, 1976) by the student of social work knowledge, skills and values cannot be promoted or achieved without critical reflection that engages with an understanding of the interplay of behaviour and values, and of societal norms and assumptions (Gardiner, 2014).

Fook (2016) argues that critical reflection has its foundation in both radical and structural theories, with critical race theory and feminism arguing that it is not the individual who is to blame but the inherently oppressive societal structures in which they live and function. Critical reflection enables the recognition of the impact of oppression (SWE, 2020) as it can uncover structural issues and imbalances of power, which will in turn demand of the student a broader understanding of social, political and legal contexts (Fook, 2016). This can only be achieved by the questioning of established practice as well as local and national policies and procedures (Gardiner, 2014). Finally, the adaptation of practice by the student to take account of the impact of oppression enhances reflective practice and enables critical reflection. Indeed, research by Sicora (2019) warns of a focus of reflection of self by social work students at the expense of reflecting on the external factors that affect the service user and service provision. Figure 4.2 illustrates the complexity of critical thinking.

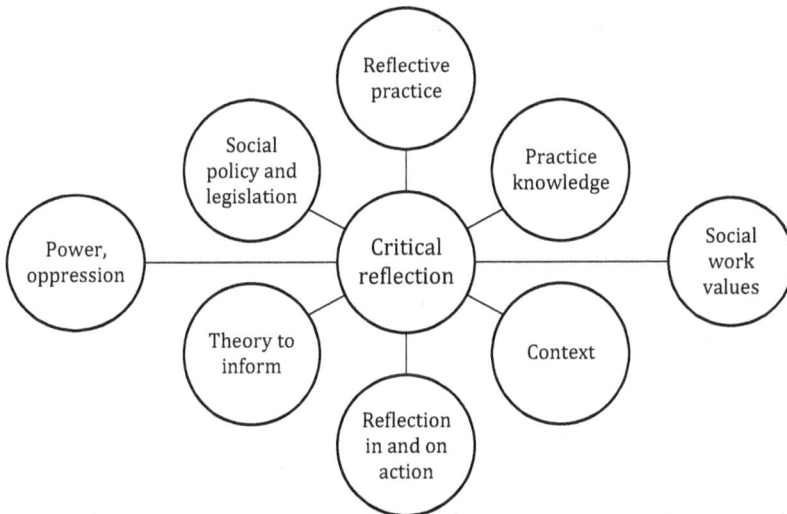

Figure 4.2 The components of critical reflection

Rolfe et al (2011) reflect that a critical thinker is one who is inquisitive and open to seeking, hearing, considering and reconsidering a range of different perspectives to ensure that they can make informed judgements based on the information available to them. This is important as it demonstrates that reflective practice relies on a range of perspectives, and also that it is not static because it is open to further reflection as new information becomes available. Indeed,

the aim of critical reflection is to assist the learner to unearth and unsettle assumptions (particularly about power) and thus to help identify a new theoretical basis from which to improve and change a practice situation.

(Fook, 2015, pp 450–4)

Clearly, this is a more complex level of reflection for a social work student to engage in and the PCF End of Last Placement (BASW, 2018) criteria expect the student to be able to '*demonstrate a capacity for logical, systematic, critical and reflective reasoning and apply the theories and techniques of reflective practice*'. This is an important distinction, as it is expected that the student will be engaging in critical reflection but they are not required to be proficient, as it is expected that the skill of critical reflection will develop within qualified practice. Nevertheless, it means that the practice educator is required to introduce critical reflection for final placement students and observe increased engagement with it as the placement progresses.

Student **development exercise**

Select an image depicting a white male. This can be taken from a magazine or internet search. Ask the student to look at the picture and tell you:

» what does the picture tell them about how the person experiences the world?

» what do they base those assumptions on?

» would the person's experiences of the world be different if they were a person of Black and global minority heritage, female or non-binary, had a hidden disability or were gay?

At first the student is likely to pick up on the physical cues within the picture: the person is happy or angry; but this should be supplemented by the practice educator asking them to explore what social norms they are basing those first impressions on. By asking them to consider the experience where the identity of the person is changed, the practice educator is stimulating discussion on the understanding of social context and the impact of societal impression on the person.

It is helpful for the practice educator to clarify the terms used within social work practice and education and through further reading become more aware of the knowledge, skills and values needed to exercise reflection at different levels. Throughout the rest of the chapter the term reflective practice will be applied in a general sense to mean the activity of experiential learning, while critical reflection will be used when discussing the concepts of context.

How to promote reflection on action

For practice educators, an essential first step early in the placement is to ascertain the student's level of understanding of reflective practice, which will in turn require the practice educator to acknowledge their own approach to reflective practice.

Professional **development prompt**

After undertaking a joint visit with a student in induction week, consider:

»   when do I reflect?

»   how do I reflect?

»   how do I take into account the service user's wishes and feelings in my reflection?

»   am I inquisitive as to why things happen?

Student **development exercise**

Ask the student to reflect on the same visit in preparation for supervision. In supervision, ask the student to:

»   reflect on how they felt about the induction visit;

»   share with you when they undertook this reflection;

»   reflect on how they felt about reflecting on the visit.

The student development exercise facilitates a diagnostic assessment of the student's reflective practice. Here it is important to remember that a non-judgemental response is critical; for example, if the student admits that they did it quickly as they were walking to supervision and the practice educator responds with criticism, the student is unlikely to offer open and honest contributions in supervision in the future. In addition, the practice educator can model their own reflection on the joint visit to demonstrate the benefits and techniques that can be used, while discussion of when and how they reflect can give the student understanding about context, personal learning styles and skills that we will seek to address later in this chapter. Finally, empathic consideration of the service user's wishes and feelings promotes understanding that reflective practice is a core component of working in partnership with people with lived experience.

We recommend you read Chapter 3 on enabling learning in parallel with this section, as the principles outlined there can be applied here to support the student to reflect on and apply knowledge to their practice to develop their skills. This section now turns to reflect on techniques that practice educators can use to engage students in developing their reflective practice, including written reflections and collaborative reflective discussion.

Written reflections

Social work students on placement are generally required to produce written reflections, which should be routinely shared with the practice educator and may form part of the academic assessment. These can come in many forms, including hand-written learning journals, printed reflective logs or electronic reflective blogs. For the purpose of this discussion, a distinction will not be made between different types of written reflection. While students may initially see written reflections as a burdensome requirement of the placement, the practice educator can develop the student's understanding to embrace written reflections as a concrete and valuable tool in experiential learning, as well as a means of making explicit their thought processes and feelings.

Reflective practice is not simply a matter of pausing for thought from time to time. Rather, it is a much more sophisticated process of integrating personal and professional knowledge with the demands of the situation as part of an intelligent and creative approach to practice.

(Thompson and Pascal, 2011, p 20)

To this end, Scragg (2019) recommends that the student invests in the development of written reflections to enhance their reflective practice. In producing their written reflections, the student may benefit from using a model of reflection or becoming habituated to responding to particular questions or prompts which should, over time, become internalised. The models of reflection are loosely based on Kolb's (1984) experiential learning model, one of the most popular being Gibbs' reflective cycle (1988) (Figure 4.3) or simplified versions of this including Driscoll's (2007) What? model of reflection (what, so what, now what?), ERA (Experience, Reflection, Action) (Jasper, 2003) and Maclean et al's (2018) SHARE model (see, hear, act, read and evaluate), to name but a few.

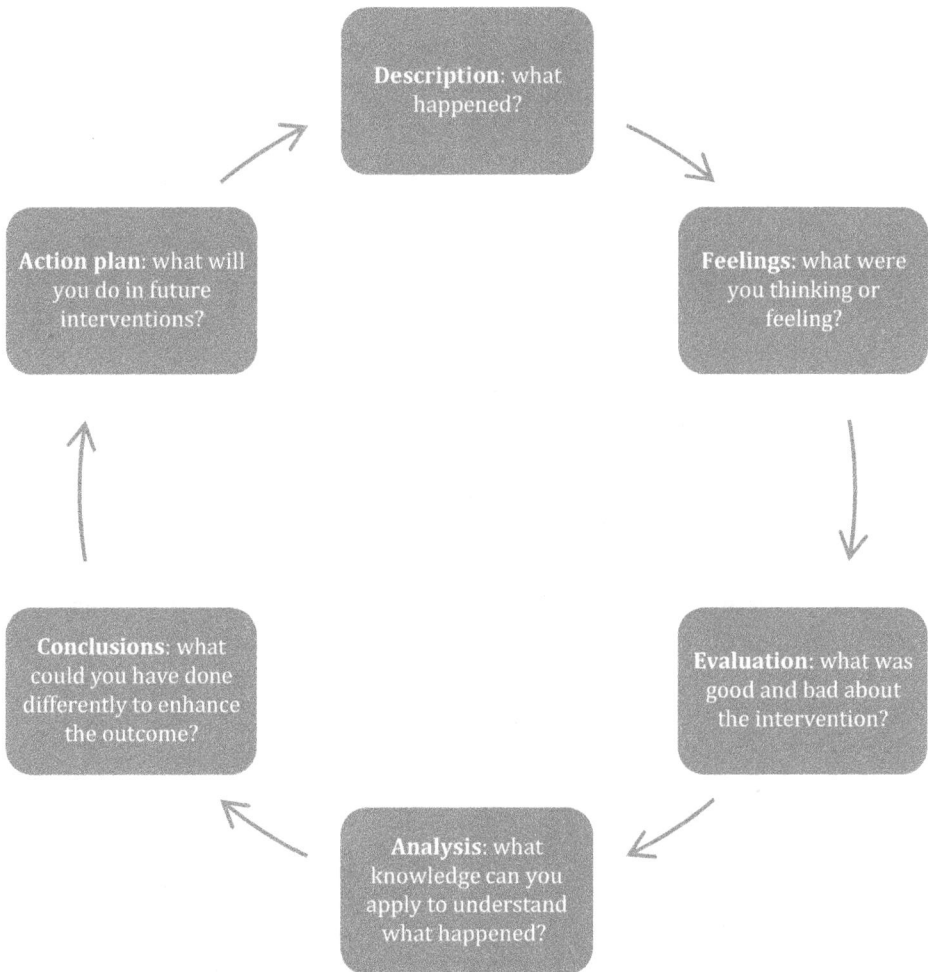

Figure 4.3 Gibbs' (1988) reflective cycle

Student **development exercise**

» Ask the student to reflect on an intervention with a service user using each of the following reflection models.

Gibbs' reflective cycle	Describe Feelings Evaluate Analyse Conclude Action plan
Maclean et al's SHARE model	See Hear Ask Read Evaluate
Driscoll's What? model	What? So what? Now what?

» In supervision, ask the student to reflect on how they found each of the models, facilitating a discussion on which one best suits their learning style.

Where the student struggles to engage with this development exercise, it can be undertaken in supervision so that the practice educator talks the student through each reflective model to facilitate a reflective discussion on which model works for the student. Where the student has a clear favourite model, encourage the student to use this model in their written reflections to develop a clear structure within which to reflect. As the student progresses through their placements, the explicit use of the model headings should be reduced, so that ultimately the student is using the model in their mind but presents a fluent written discussion on paper.

The completion of a written reflection is likely to take some time, since, as Ingham (2015, p 75) notes, the student should '*reflect, edit, prioritise, and present an account of their practice*'. It is unlikely that the first draft of a written reflection will be the final draft, but it is often a good basis on which to base further discussion of the student's ideas. Indeed, the production of written reflections should not be seen as purely a student task: the practice educator's role within written reflections is critical in developing the student's reflective practice. The practice educator should provide constructive feedback on the written reflection to enhance the student's understanding of what can be included in a written reflection or to prompt further reflection. For example, the sentence *'Mrs F was angry at me'* could invite feedback that it could be enhanced in a number of ways, including an empathic reflection on why Mrs F was angry, for example, was it about the student's practice and/ or was it Mrs F's experiences of being an oppressed and marginalised vulnerable person in an able society? In addition, the use of different highlighter pen colours can illustrate how much each task in the model has been used; for example, a proliferation of pink indicating description at the expense of green indicating application of theory can be a powerful exercise for the student to appreciate an unbalanced reflection.

It is important to remember that a written reflection should be nuanced, which can be difficult when writing within often quite limited word counts. The practice educator may need to offer support to the student on what content to include and exclude, as well as on a concise style of writing. Nevertheless, written reflection should include, across the breadth of the placement, the student's emotional reaction to the event, the theory and policy that underpin and/or explain the event, the student's values, identification of social contexts and oppression, as well as exploring differing perspectives of people with lived experience and the priorities of different service provisions.

Finally, the exploration of ethical dilemmas within a written reflection can help the student to explore their own opinion or perspective where they were unclear, in a similar way to writing a pros and cons list to help make a decision. It is important to remember here that within social work there are often multiple right answers: Ingham (2015) reminds us that written reflections are subjective and are the thoughts of the writer. The practice educator is not looking for the correct answer but instead for evidence that the student is an open, critical thinker.

Collaborative reflective discussion

Chapter 5 sets out detail about social work student supervision, where collaborative reflective discussion forms a significant part of the process as is outlined in the reflective learning model (Davys and Beddoe, 2009); that chapter should be read in conjunction with this section. Collaborative reflective discussion takes the student's initial reflective ideas and develops them further as the practice educator asks stimulating questions that require the student to think beyond their initial reflection. The use of framing questions (who, why, what, where, when, how) can facilitate a reflective approach (Brockbank and McGill, 2007). This may be an easy way for uncertain students to approach reflection.

Case **example**

When discussing a new service user (Hilda), the practice educator identifies that the student, Zoe, is struggling to reflect on the key issues. The practice educator asks Zoe framing questions to stimulate her thinking.

» Who could you contact to support your understanding of Hilda?

» Who does Hilda identify as a support for themselves?

» Why have we received a referral?

» Why might Hilda be reluctant to engage with our service?

» What is the framework and plan for intervention?

» What might happen if you...?

» Where will the intervention take place and what planning have you taken to ensure that you are ready for the appointment?

» When will you ask for support?

» When will you know that you have gathered the appropriate information within the initial assessment?

» How do you think you will approach your first appointment with Hilda?

Reflect on these framing questions and consider which you would use in a similar discussion. Can you identify other framing questions that you would prefer?

This may read as more of interrogation of Zoe than a reflective discussion, which is clearly not the intention. However, by having these questions in mind, the practice educator is able to supplement the student's reflection and stimulate where she is stuck in her reflection.

An interesting reflective model comes from the field of Japanese car manufacture, called the Five Whys (Ohno, 1950s), where cause and effect are seen as a method of understanding to develop solutions.

Case **example (continued)**

The practice educator reflects on the initial assessment of Hilda with Zoe.

1. *PE: Why are you feeling that the visit with Hilda went well?*
   Student: Because she engaged with me and I got lots of important information from her.

2. *PE: Why did she engage with you?*
   Student: Because I listened to her. I think I took a person-centred approach with her and made her feel that I respected her.

3. *PE: Why is it important that she felt respected?*
   Student: Because she may have been feeling a sense of loss for her independence and that can be really hard.

4. *PE: Why do you apply theories of loss here?*
   Student: Because it just seemed apt. The referral said she had low mood and used to be a really active person, so I wondered if it might be the case.

5. *PE: Why do you think understanding loss enhances your empathy skills?*
   Student: Umm, that's a good question. I think probably because if I can understand how Hilda might be feeling, I am more sensitive to recognising it and can adjust my communication to ensure I meet her needs, which I guess is why the meeting went well.

» Can you think of some different 'why?' questions that could stimulate Zoe and perhaps take the discussion down a different reflective discussion route?

To any reader who has cared for a young child, the case example will remind them of the developmental stage. However, it is important that we acknowledge that the purpose of this exercise is the way in which the child acquires understanding of their environment. The questions that the practice educator asks within the reflective discussion stimulate the student's knowledge and skills.

Secondly, collaborative reflective discussion enables the practice educator to share their practice wisdom with the student, thus enhancing the student's knowledge that can be applied to the reflection and development of skills. Argyris and Schön (1974) focus on reflective discussion, which they define as an open and honest discussion that respects each other's views that new thinking and learning can occur for students as they develop ideas through discussion and reflection. As they state, '*every attempt to try new behaviour is reinforced by the instructor*' (Argyris and Schön, 1974, p 128). Likewise, diagrammatic exercises can assist the student to develop their reflective skills, which engage the visual learner (Fleming, 2001). These can include:

Mind mapping: where a service user or intervention is chosen for reflection and located in the centre of a large piece of paper. Initial ideas, topics and themes are added around the service user or intervention and then each idea is developed with sub-ideas and so on, thus developing the reflection.

SWOT analysis: the student is asked to complete a square with four sections to include their Strengths and Weaknesses in relation to a social work skill, and to identify any Opportunities and Threats to the development of the skills.

The use of collaborative reflective discussion enhances the student's reflection on their self, provides a different perspective to stimulate further reflection, and enables the student to benefit from the practice educator's practice wisdom and knowledge of social work theory. In so doing, it enhances the development of the student's knowledge and skills.

Reflection on social work values

While on placement, the student is required to develop their social work values and ethics (PCF, D2), as well as their understanding of diversity and oppression (PCF, D3) and human rights and social justice (PCF, D4) (BASW, 2018). Social work students are required to reflect on – and understand the roots of – oppression and social injustice, on the authority held through the power invested in the role of social worker and be able to take steps to address and reduce power differentials on a personal and community level. The practice educator's role is, as with all social work knowledge and skills, to teach and assess the student's development in these domains. However, the practice educator is also required to challenge any oppressive practice or judgemental attitudes on the part of the student to enhance their reflection on self.

An awareness of one's values and beliefs, and their impact on practice, is a fundamental expectation of social work education. Learning to understand the role that values play in social work practice is a significant aspect of placement for students, and often one of the most challenging. This can be an area where students feel at their most vulnerable and may struggle with articulating and reflecting on their own value base. The power differential between practice educator and student can be heightened as students fear that revealing '*wrong*' values may impair their ability to be assessed positively. In order to maximise the potential for constructive reflective discussion, an open and honest climate needs to be established in which sometimes difficult areas of assumptions, prejudices, values, beliefs and ethical questions can be examined, reflected upon and accommodated into professional development. Furthermore, the practice educator must also be prepared to be vulnerable and to model the exploration of values, ethics, oppression, discrimination, human rights and social justice honestly.

Models can be extraordinarily helpful in understanding a range of topics, none more so than when considering social work values and anti-oppressive practice. Models engage the visual learner and reduce the need to provide an immediate response within an often extensive and ambiguous topic discussion such as '*how were your values challenged here?*', as they facilitate directed reflection and can be used to develop the student's understanding of social work values. Social work values require the student to see the service user as an individual and respond to their unique strengths and needs. This comes from an understanding of their identity, which is multi-faceted and complex. In order to prompt the student's reflection on service user identity, the social GGRRAAACCEEESSS model (Burnham, 2012) can be considered.

Student **development exercise**

In supervision, ask the student to reflect on a person with whom they are working and reflect on how their identity impacts on them positively in relation to:

» gender;	» abilities;	» education;
» geography;	» appearance;	» employment;
» race;	» culture;	» sexuality;
» religion;	» class;	» sexual orientation;
» age;	» ethnicity;	» spirituality.

It is important that the student does not make assumptions about the person with lived experiences because of their identity, but instead listens to their experiences. Here, the student is asked to take a strengths-based approach to identify the skills and resources that the person can build upon to engage with service provision. By repeating the exercise and replacing '*how their identity impacts on them positively*' with the '*discrimination they face as a result of their identity*', the student will also be able to reflect upon the oppression that the service user may face in order to develop an understanding of the intersectionality of oppression. Finally, this is an exercise that a student could be directed to undertake *with* the service user to enable deep learning about the impact of oppression on people with lived experience. The practice educator would need to ensure that the service user was prepared for the exercise and willing to participate with the student.

Critical reflection

Where the student is progressing further, perhaps in the latter half of the first placement or in the final placement, the practice educator will support the student to develop their reflective practice by adding critical reflection to their existing skills. Brookfield (2017) argues that the key components of critical thinking are identifying and questioning assumptions, which enable the student to explore and enact different responses that address power and oppression. In order to be able to support the student to develop the skill of critical reflection, you must first identify if you are critically reflective, which returns us to the professional development prompt at the start of this section: are you inquisitive? Many social workers remain politically and socially aware and critically reflective; however, for some social workers this may have slipped due to a complex caseload and stress levels, deprioritising it as a social work skill. Here the practice educator is asked to model critical reflection and awareness of the context in which social work practice takes place, so that they can model and discuss critical reflection with the student. In addition, a number of activities can be undertaken with the student to stimulate their critical reflection.

It is important to reflect that the student is likely to be working with the most vulnerable people in society, who are often further impacted by social issues such as poverty. The student development exercise below is a good one to undertake with the student to encourage reflection on their values in relation to the impact of the poverty and oppression.

Student **development exercise**

In supervision, ask the student to reflect on how poverty:

» has and is affecting them;

» might be affecting the service users they are working with.

Can the student identify the impact of poverty on mental health, etc?

This exercise aims to facilitate a collaborative reflective discussion that firstly develops the practice educator's understanding of the student in order to be able to offer support if required and secondly to develop an empathic discussion that develops the student's knowledge, skills and values in relation to service provision.

The PCS analysis model (Thompson, 1997) is a seminal model that requires exploration of the **P**ersonal, **C**ultural and **S**tructural discrimination that a person with lived experience encounters and how this may impact on their ability to engage with service provision.

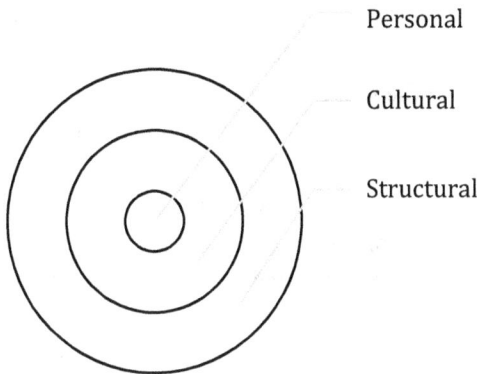

Personal

Cultural

Structural

Figure 4.4 PCS model (Thompson, 1997)

Student **development exercise**

» In supervision, ask the student to reflect on a home visit to a person who is experiencing domestic abuse and consider how each of these aspects influenced the intervention.

When considering the personal, ask the student to reflect on how they felt about the woman: is this any different to how they felt about the perpetrator? When working with a student at the start of the first placement, they may express stereotypical responses to the personal level of discrimination, including frustration that the woman has not left the home or anger along the lines of '*all men are evil*'. These form an excellent basis for a discussion about personal and professional values, which can lead into a debate about the social construction of cultural discrimination and assumptions and how they can have an impact on intervention delivery and need to be further reflected upon to develop social work values. Finally, the practice educator can direct the student through a discussion about the impact of legislation, social policy and lack of resources that prevent the woman from being able to engage in meaningful service provision that could empower her to have choice and control in her life as to how the situation is resolved.

The SHARP framework (Shaia, 2019) provides the student with a way to understand the oppression that a service user has experienced and is experiencing. The model enables an empathic understanding of the person's ability to engage with service provision, and this can lead to solutions that engage them appropriately to meet their individual needs, taking an informed person-centred approach. The SHARP framework requires the student to consider the impact of **S**tructural oppression and **H**istorical context, thus considering the impact that poverty, limited education and employment opportunities, and poor housing options have had and continue to have on their health, ability to engage with services, and relationship with the social worker. This is then followed by an **A**nalysis of the social worker's role, and reflection on the impact of self within the intervention, which can include institutional and interpersonal oppression. Importantly, **R**eciprocity and mutuality engages them where their wishes and feelings, and an understanding of their own needs and strengths, can be used to address areas for development, as well as limitations, as these are heard and taken account of by the student. Finally, the student should reflect on the **P**ower that their role affords them and how they can work collaboratively with service users to empower them to engage with service provision and enhance their outcomes. However, this should also include the student supporting the person to be equipped with the skills to enable them to address future oppression.

Student **development exercise**

In supervision, ask the student to reflect on a home visit to a service user from a Black and global minority (BGM) and consider the impact that each of the following had on the intervention:

» structural oppression;

» historical context;

» analysis of role;

» reciprocity and mutuality;

» power.

The student should then reflect on how they can empower the person in each area, thus developing a plan of intervention for the coming period. This can be reviewed in a future supervision session to reflect on progress.

This can be a powerful exercise to undertake with the student, and perhaps a little more directed than Thompson's PCS model, thus facilitating a more directed reflective discussion.

Tedam (2021) provides a framework for reflection and discussion in relation to oppressive practice that can be used equally by the practice educator on their own practice but it is exemplified here as a student development exercise. There are parallels with the experiential learning cycle (Kolb, 1984) that was discussed above, as the student is asked to reflect on an incident, develop a theoretical understanding, make an action plan and apply the learning. The framework requires the student to reflect on the **P**ower and **P**rivilege that impacts the service user through **D**iscussion with them about their experiences of oppression. This leads to a reflection on self and service delivery and the **D**iscovery that, despite a commitment to anti-oppressive and anti-discriminatory practice, there are still areas for development where practice can be enhanced, in order to **D**ecide on an action plan to develop own practice or challenge service delivery practice, which is enacted to **D**isrupt the oppressive practice and enhance good practice.

Student **development exercise**

In supervision, ask the student to consider their power and privilege within an intervention with a service user with a learning disability through the following reflective process:

» discuss;

» discover;

» decide;

» disrupt.

The student could ask the service user for feedback prior to the supervision session to inform the reflective discussion within supervision. The student should be able to discover new perspectives on their ability, their role as social worker, and the disabling role of society, which could lead to creative ways in which the student could decide and plan to empower service users in the future. In the following supervision session, the student could reflect on the impact of the disruption on oppressive practices and enhancement of good practices.

The Theory Circle (Collingwood, 2005), as discussed in Chapter 3, can be revisited to ensure reflection on the student's application of theory to their understanding of the intervention, thus developing their ability to identify, understand and address the issues of power and oppression that the person may face.

Critical incident analysis (Green and Crisp, 2007) can be used to focus on issues and dilemmas in relation to power, inequality, oppression and exclusion within the following model:

» account of the incident;

» initial response to the incident;

» issues and dilemmas highlighted by the incident;

» learning;

» outcome.

The critical reflection process (Fook, 2016) first requires that the student presents an intervention, describing what happens. This is followed by an analytical stage, where the student is facilitated to explore the contexts and hidden assumptions that have impacted the intervention, including oppression, power and discrimination. Finally, the student is supported to reflect on how the hidden assumptions impact their practice and how they can address the power differentials to enhance service user outcomes.

Furthermore, revisiting the framing questions introduced earlier in this chapter can provide a good basis for the practice educator, but at this stage with more of a focus on the context of the intervention.

» Who determines the service provision service criteria? Do they come from a managerial, financial or service user-led perspective?

» Why did the service user respond in that way to your intervention?

» What sort of language did you use and what impact did it have?

» Where did you assert your power and what sort of power do you think it was?

» When do your personal values impact your professional values and do they impact your service provision?

» How has your thinking changed, and what might you do differently now?

Finally, it should be noted that students will be required to be critically reflective in order to undertake assessments within their placement. There are a number of excellent books available on assessment writing, and the practice educator is directed to them to engage the student with the knowledge and skills required for that task.

How to promote reflection in action

In the previous section, the practice educator was encouraged to develop practical strategies to support the student's development of reflection on action, which is commonly perceived as a student's reflection. In this section, reflection in action is discussed. Reflection in action is a more responsive style of reflection that informs the student's social work practice and decision making within the intervention. Reflection in action requires the transferability of social work knowledge and skills, and as such requires the student to draw on previous experience to inform current activity. Ferguson (2018) argues that social workers use reflection in action to analyse and modify their practice within an intervention, but that their ability to do this can be compromised by their anxiety within the intervention. The practice educator's role here is to support the student to develop a commitment to developing the knowledge, skills and values that will enable them to be able to reflect in action. This section includes reflective practice in action and decision making.

Reflective practice in action

Reflective practice, as discussed above, is the self-identification of the student's strengths and areas for development. It is aided by the use of a reflective model that promotes the application of theory to reflection on practice. Where the student is undertaking reflective practice in action, it is often framed by thoughts such as '*that didn't engage her; what can I do to engage her?*' It is important here that reflective practice in action does not become a barrier to listening (Beesley et al, 2018), where the student is disabled by their focus on what they should do next, rather than a focus on the service user. The following may help the student to anticipate problems that might arise in an intervention, but could also enable the practice educator to identify solutions.

Student **development activity**

In supervision, when planning and reflecting on an intervention with Hilda from the case example above, ask the student a series of '*what if?*' questions designed to prepare the student's ability to reflect in action, for example:

» What if Hilda wouldn't answer your questions?

» What if Hilda shouted at you to leave?

» What if Hilda really liked you and didn't want you to leave after an hour?

Each of these questions can be seen to catastrophise the planned visit, so it is important that you explain that the purpose of the activity is to prepare the student and not to terrify them! It may not be appropriate for all students to undertake, and the importance of understanding your student is reiterated here (Beesley, 2022). However, by identifying potential problems, you can develop solutions that the student could apply if they occurred, thus enhancing their ability to reflect in action during the intervention. Furthermore, this student development activity can also be used after an intervention to stimulate the reluctant-to-reflect student by hypothetically changing one aspect of the situation. This is done in order to help the student think more broadly about their practice as it may be more accessible for the active learner (Honey and Mumford, 1992) or kinaesthetic learner (Fleming, 2001) to engage with.

Similarly, role plays can prepare the student for a forthcoming intervention as they can practise their responses to the service user; role plays also enable modelling of the social work skill by the practice educator. An additional aspect of learning from role plays is that students develop empathy for the person, which inevitably enhances their ability to engage in reflective practice.

However, it is important to prepare the student for the fact that, regardless of the preparation undertaken for an intervention, social workers work with real people, and therefore their responses will be unpredictable. Reflection in action may result in the student needing support after the intervention, and a debriefing session will enable them to reflect on action on the reflection in action.

Decision making

Leonard and O'Connor (2018) identified that social workers progress through three stages as they develop their decision-making skills: 'outsider observer', 'inside player' and 'inside expert player' roles, recognising that the social work student is not expected to progress to the third stage until further into their career. This section provides the practice educator with tools to support the student to undertake the journey from 'outsider observer' to 'insider expert'.

Student **development exercise**

Ask the student to reflect on making a decision in their personal life, for example, what to have for tea.

» How did the student make the decision?

This student development exercise is designed to demonstrate to the student that they make everyday decisions which require them to reflect in action. They may have identified that they thought about what they like to eat, so they drew on their knowledge from past experiences, but also considered what was available to them to eat, who else was eating with them and what they wanted to eat or if they had any allergies. The practice educator's role here is to take the student slowly through the process to demonstrate their strengths in decision making, perhaps using the framing questions introduced above to further their reflection. Once this has been completed, ask the student to repeat the exercise but with a simple decision that they have made on placement, finally asking them to consider how this differs from the personal decision-making process.

Another activity that the practice educator could undertake with the student to develop their social work skills is process recording. While this has fallen out of favour because it is time-consuming and is not currently used for everyday case recording, it remains a good teaching tool.

Student **development exercise**

»   Ask the student to write a detailed account of an intervention imme-diately after it occurs, ensuring that they included everything that happened in the appointment, however trivial. In supervision, go through the process recording, and at each point ask the student why they responded in the way they did or what made them choose to say that, at that time and in that way.

The purpose of this activity is to develop the student's understanding of why they made the decision to respond in the way they did, to make them more aware of their decision-making processes and to identify their strengths. Furthermore, Mullin and Canning (2007) identified that using process recording with social work students enhances their understanding of the work undertaken and enhances service provision.

The following decision-making checklist provides an outline that they can follow when reflecting on action.

1.   Determine the decision to be made.

2.   Ensure that all relevant and available information is collected.

3.   Consider the potential impact of the decision.

4.   Consider any biases.

5.   Communicate the decision and act on it.

6.   Reflect on the outcome.

This list can be used in the exercise to determine which stages they engage with and whether particular stages need to be developed to support the student's ability to make decisions and reflect in action. When decision making, the student will draw on a variety of different aspects of knowledge. The first will be the transferability of knowledge and skills from a previous intervention and reflection, as the student will use what they already know. All decisions made about the service user should include their wishes and feelings and take account of the impact that all potential decisions will have on them. O'Sullivan (2011) reminds us of the importance of involving the service user in decision making, and thus the importance of reflection in action. This should then be supplemented with the service provision context of social policy, legislation and agency procedures, as well as theories to inform and to intervene (Collingwood, 2005), and an understanding of social work values and power and the impact that they have had and will have on the person. Indeed, decision making should personify critical reflection, where the social worker very quickly takes account of a wide range of issues.

Conclusion

This chapter has explored how reflective practice frames and holds together the student's development of knowledge, skills and values. The true skill of an effective practice educator lies in unlocking the responses of a student to their experiences and in so doing promotes a reflective approach to learning and improving practice, which results in enhanced service provision for people with lived experience. Critical reflection is seen to take the reflective practice on the student's self and further layer in a criticality that takes account of the cultural and structural factors that impact on service provision. Critical reflection, as exemplified in Figure 4.2, should take account of the student's strengths and areas for development in their reflective practice, which requires an understanding of the theories applied to enhance understanding and consequently skill development; this is set within an understanding of power, oppression and social work values.

While this chapter has focused on how the practice educator supports the student to develop their reflective practice and social work values, it is pertinent to remind the practice educator that they too should be reflectively practice educating. It is hoped that the practice educator will pay attention to their own ability to engage in critical reflection and to create space and energy for this most important of activities alongside their student. Indeed, while the principles of good practice in experiential learning require a self-aware and critically reflective student, this is enhanced by the assistance of a practice educator who is constantly reflecting upon and reviewing learning opportunities and development of knowledge, skills and values.

Taking it further

Banks, S (2021) *Ethics and Values in Social Work*. London: Red Globe Press. A well-established book on this topic. The Introduction and Chapter 2 in particular are useful for looking at the difference between values and ethics and considering the role of the social worker politically and ethically in society. Useful case studies illustrate the arguments put forward.

Beckett, C, Maynard, A and Jordan, P (2017) *Values and Ethics in Social Work*. London: Sage. This book provides accessible discussion on social work values.

Doel, M (2016) *Rights and Wrongs in Social Work: Ethical and Practice Dilemmas*. London: Palgrave. This book provides excellent case studies to use in supervision with a student to develop their understanding of ethical dilemmas.

Fook, J (2016) *Social Work: A Critical Approach to Practice*. London: Sage. This seminal book looks at critical social work and provides ideas for developing reflective practice.

Ingram, R (2015) *Understanding Emotions in Social Work: Theory, Practice and Reflection*. Maidenhead: Open University Press. Chapter 3 of this book locates emotional intelligence as important to promote reflection.

Mantell, A and Scragg, T (eds) (2019) *Reflective Practice in Social Work*. London: Sage. This edited book provides a strong range of discussions on reflective practice that can be helpfully accessed by the practice educator to share and discuss with the student. Chapter 1 is particularly useful as a review of the development and relevance of reflective practice in social work. Chapter 8 focuses on reflective practice on placement.

Tedam, P (2021) *Anti-oppressive Social Work Practice*. London: Sage. An excellent book that explores all areas of anti-oppressive practice and includes a chapter on placement provision.

Thompson, N (2021) *Anti-discriminatory Practice: Equality, Diversity and Social Justice*. London: Red Globe Press. This is the newest edition of Thompson's classic that introduced the PCS model and considers it in the light of contemporary issues.

Chapter aims

» To consider different models of supervision and how they may be applied in supervision with a student.

» To examine how supervision is structured and what skills, techniques and approaches are helpful for practice educators to use during supervision.

» To reflect on ways to reduce the power differential in social work student supervision.

Critical **questions**

» How will you maintain the balance between the differing functions of supervision and ensure that the needs of the service user, the student and the organisation are met?

» How can your own professional supervision be extended to incorporate and support your role as a practice educator of social work students?

Introduction

This chapter will meet many of the Practice Educator Professional Standards for social work (PEPS) domains (BASW, 2022), as supervision has a multi-function purpose (Doel, 2010).

While on placement, students should have regular supervision with a practice educator (SWE, 2019; BASW, 2022). Supervision plays an essential role within the placement, as it is a forum for the development of students' knowledge, skills and values; support for students; case management discussion to enable accountability; and an opportunity for the practice educator to develop formative assessment of the social work student.

Recent reviews of social work education recommended that the quality of social work student supervision be promoted as a site of development (Croisdale-Appleby, 2014; Narey, 2014).

It is the quality of the placement and the supervision received that is most frequently cited both by students and recently qualified social workers as key in the initial formation of their own professional practice – it is that important!

(Croisdale-Appleby, 2014, p 49)

Social work supervision is valued for its positive impact on service provision by organisations and practitioners alike (Wonnacott, 2012; Kadushin and Harkness, 2014; Lawler, 2015; SCIE, 2017), yet successive reports (Laming, 2003, 2009; Munro, 2011; Croisdale-Appleby, 2014; Narey, 2014) have highlighted that many social workers and social work students have received inadequate, poor-quality supervision and that supervision has often been dominated by managerial demands. The publication of the Knowledge and Skills Statements (KSS) for practice supervisors (DfE, 2018) of children's social workers also reiterated the need for supervisors to strike an appropriate balance between case management and reflective supervision.

Indeed, research has identified that students associated placement satisfaction with learning within supervision (Kanno and Koeske, 2010; Roulston et al, 2018; Wilson and Flanagan, 2021). However, neither the practice educators' guidance (BASW, 2022) nor the social work education guidance (SWE, 2019) specified good practice in relation to social work student supervision. Of note is that Simmonds (2018) found that individual supervisors utilised different styles of supervising, indicating a flexibility of styles and models of supervision, many of which will be outlined within this chapter. Furthermore, research into the practice education role within supervision, and the role of supervision more generally, has highlighted the importance that supervision plays in assisting learning and professional development (Jasper and Field, 2016; Cleak et al, 2016; Ketner et al, 2017) and the role of supervision in enhancing emotional health and resilience (Ingram, 2013, 2015; Grant and Kinman, 2013), which will be further discussed in this chapter. However, while the emphasis will be on how the practice educator can provide effective supervision for a social work student, it should not be forgotten that students too have a responsibility to engage with their own learning (Knowles, 1973) within supervision.

For our purposes in this chapter, when we refer to 'supervision' we are referring to formal, planned supervision sessions taking place on a one-to-one basis between the practice educator and the student. Social work student supervision

can offer a formal space for students to explore fears, anxieties, emotions and feelings... offers a forum for learning, ensures that both students and service users are kept safe, and provides opportunities for students to demonstrate their learning to enable the practice educator to make an holistic assessment of their knowledge, skills and ability.

(Dix, 2018, p 43)

This is different to informal supervision, which the student may seek on an ad hoc basis from the practice educator or other members of the team and usually has a problem-solving focus. It is important that informal supervision does not become the dominant form of practice educator and student interaction as it is less focused on the educational aspect of supervision and often does not afford the student a confidential space to explore in-depth complex issues. Finally, it is essential that any decision taken, or advice given informally, is then referred to and recorded during the next formal supervision session. In addition, there are other forms of supervision, such as group supervision and peer supervision, but these are not the focus of this chapter.

This chapter reflects on social work student supervision theory, including the functional model of supervision (Kadushin, 1976; Doel, 2010), the reflective learning model (Davys and Beddoe, 2009) and the 4×4×4 integrated model of supervision (Morrison, 2005). The chapter also considers the processes of supervision, including the supervision life cycle, supervision agreement, confidentiality, supervision structure and supervision minutes. The chapter ends with a discussion on the MANDELA model, and the impact that the supervisory relationship and collaborative supervision can have on reducing the power imbalance.

Supervision models

There are a number of different social work student supervision models available, and this chapter begins with a discussion of the functional model of supervision (Kadushin, 1976; Doel, 2010), the reflective learning model (Davys and Beddoe, 2009) and the 4×4×4 integrated model of supervision (Morrison, 2005).

Functions of supervision

Originally based on the supervision of qualified social workers, Kadushin (1976) created the functional model of supervision, which Doel (2010) developed to include the assessment function for student supervision. There are four related but separate elements to social work student supervision, which are referred to by the acronym ESMA, as follows:

> **E**ducation function;
>
> **S**upport function;
>
> **M**anagement function;
>
> **A**ssessment function.

It is clear how three of these functions relate to the main areas of the practice educator role – support, management of the placement and the education and teaching element – but it is also important to remember how supervision contributes to the assessment of the student, which will be discussed in greater detail in Chapter 6. It is impossible to have a case management discussion without providing education through theoretical understanding, procedural knowledge, practice wisdom and student support, while also assessing the student's initial and developing knowledge and reaction to the supervision discussion. If the practice educator's engagement with all functions are reflected upon and developed, the PEPS (BASW, 2022) Domain D *'developing knowledge and continuing performance as a practice educator'* will be met.

Education

The first function in the ESMA supervision model is that of education. This is the function of supervision that is concerned with learning and the development of knowledge, skills and values against which the student will be assessed. Indeed, if one returns to the PCF (BASW, 2018) the student is required to develop skills in all nine domains. Chapter 3 provides an excellent discussion of enabling learning and the student development exercises in each chapter provide practice education tools that can be used by practice educators with students to enhance learning.

In demonstrating the education function in supervision with a student, the practice educator will meet many of the PEPS (BASW, 2022) Domain B criteria *'teaching, facilitating and supporting learning and professional development in practice'*.

Support

Supervision should be a source of support for students, as an arena for managing the emotional impact of working with vulnerable people and also an opportunity for the student to receive support in managing the demands of their professional training and the university/placement/assessment/life balance. Supervision should thus be a place where students can be helped to recognise and acknowledge the emotional impact of working with vulnerable or challenging service users. In circumstances where the emotional impact of the work with service users is experienced as overwhelming, or if the student has personal issues that are impacting on the placement, they can be acknowledged and discussed to a degree during supervision; but any further help, support or counselling has to be accessed outside the placement and the student should be encouraged to seek further support from their tutor or specific support services offered within the university. It is important to remember that any social work student should be fit to practice, and subject to both professional and university guidelines.

However, the supportive function of supervision extends beyond the attention given to the well-being of the student and is also seen as an important function in supporting the student to engage with and access the learning in a manner that is student centred.

In supporting a student, the practice educator will meet many of the PEPS (BASW, 2022) Domain B criteria *'teaching, facilitating and supporting learning and professional development in practice'*.

Management

This function of supervision is concerned with the quality assurance aspect of a placement and ensuring that the student is working in accordance with national standards, legislation, and any agency policy and procedures. The key aim of this function is to safeguard the protection and safety of service users and carers. This will involve ensuring the student's accountability for their work on placement and their understanding and adherence to agency requirements, for example, in relation to key processes; case recording requirements; safeguarding; and health and safety.

It is important to remember that management takes account of the context of the work undertaken by the student; thus, the management function should include discussion about both procedural and legislative expectations, as well as the needs of the service user (Dix, 2018). Case management discussion in supervision can facilitate the development of the student's empathic responses and understanding of the impact of oppression, thus enhancing practice and service user outcomes.

The managerial aspect of student supervision also includes management of the placement itself and managing the demands of both the professional framework that the student is working within and those of the education provider. For example, this includes working with the student to help them understand their assessment requirements, and agreeing with the student key learning objectives to be met by certain points in the placement.

In fulfilling the management function, the practice educator will be meeting many of the requirements of Domain A of the PEPS (BASW, 2022) *'work with others to organise an effective learning environment'*.

Assessment

The assessment of students is covered in significant detail in Chapter 6. However, it is important to reflect here that assessment is a holistic activity for practice educators, rather than an assessment event. While the importance of direct observation of practice is recognised along with the need to meet the placement assessment criteria, it is also acknowledged that reflective discussion in supervision provides material for the formative assessment by the practice educator, enabling them to adjust the level of support and education provided to meet the student's individual learning needs.

In demonstrating the assessment function, the practice educator will be meeting many of the requirements of Domain C of the PEPS (BASW, 2022) *'manage the fair and transparent assessment of students in practice'*.

Professional **development prompt**

Consider the functions of supervision: education, support, management and assessment.

» What *'weight'* should be given to each?

» How will you ensure that *'managerial'* considerations do not dominate?

The reflective learning model

Thus far we have asked the reader to consider the different functions that they will carry out with the student within supervision. We now turn our attention to a model that advocates a reflective approach to social work student supervision, the reflective learning model (Davys and Beddoe, 2009). This model focuses on the process of supervision and describes a four-stage cycle of supervision that closely follows Kolb's (1984) cycle of experiential learning with specific tasks at each stage for supervisor and supervisee. However, it is supplemented by the concept of reflective discussion (Argyris and Schön, 1974), where an open and honest discussion that respects each other's views develops ideas, or *'two heads are better than one'*. This new thinking and learning can occur for students as they develop ideas through reflective discussion. Reflective discussion can create a greater sense of connectedness between participants; reduce power differentials (Hair, 2014); stimulate a greater sense of openness to learning (Fook, 2015); and enhance outcomes for service users, as the social worker is better placed to be able to understand and explain the socially constructed oppression and social justice issues the service user experiences (Rankine et al, 2018), which is a core social work value.

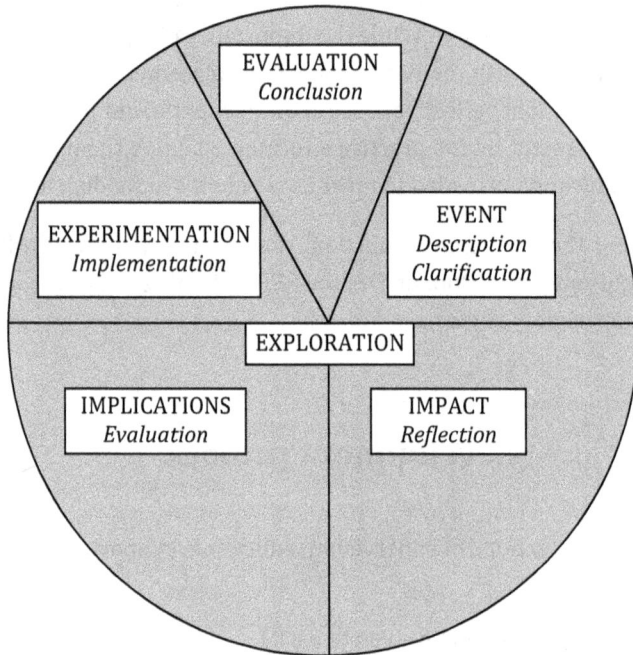

Figure 5.1 The reflective learning model: supervision of social work students. © Davys and Beddoe (2009)

Davys and Beddoe (2009) argue that this model helps to promote reflection in the *'exploration'* stage but also the concept of learning from both successes and mistakes in the *'experimentation'* and the *'evaluation'* stage. The stages comprise the following.

>> **The event** – the student is encouraged to explain the event or interaction with the service user so that both the supervisor and supervisee gain a clear understanding of the issue.

>> **Exploration** – this is the stage where the work of supervision takes place (Davys and Beddoe, 2009). It is divided into two phases: impact and implications. Firstly, the impact of the event on the student and the service user is discussed and the student's own role in it is discussed. The second phase is exploration of the implications, which involves the student and

practice educator together considering the case more broadly to include the legislation, policies and theories that can inform and guide future action. The aim of the exploration stage is to increase understanding, insight and knowledge, and is a collaborative combination of student-led ideas and practice educator-led questions to prompt further discussion and information sharing to develop student knowledge and understanding (Beesley, 2022).

» **Experimentation** – the exploration stage should result in developing a plan on how the student will approach future planned work so that they can enhance both their skills and service provision. This requires the exploration of a variety of models of intervention, with empathic and emotionally intelligent discussion that develops the student's understanding of the impact of service provision on the service user.

» **Evaluation** – this is the stage where the practice educator checks with the student that they have understood what has been agreed. It will require a supervision discussion that reflects on what knowledge, support or resources the student may need to enable them to undertake the work.

When all stages of the reflective learning model have been completed, the student and practice educator will focus on the next agenda item and begin the cycle once more. Beyond its use as a model of supervision, this model may also help students in preparing any written critically reflective analyses of their practice.

The 4×4×4 integrated model of supervision

Supervision takes place within a particular context and is not simply a relationship between two people but is a '*multifaceted relationship*' (Tsui, 2005, p 41) that involves the supervisor, supervisee, service user, the agency and the wider cultural context. Within social work student supervision, the *context* also involves the team, the university, the assessment criteria (Professional Capability Framework – PCF) (BASW, 2018), the Professional Standards (SWE, 2019) that guide practice expectations, and the PEPS (BASW, 2022) that guide practice education practice.

Morrison (2005) identified that social work supervision is a complex event that takes account of a wide range of issues. He developed the 4×4×4 integrated model of supervision to recognise the complexity of supervision, including the range of tasks, stakeholders and functions and how they are interconnected within supervision.

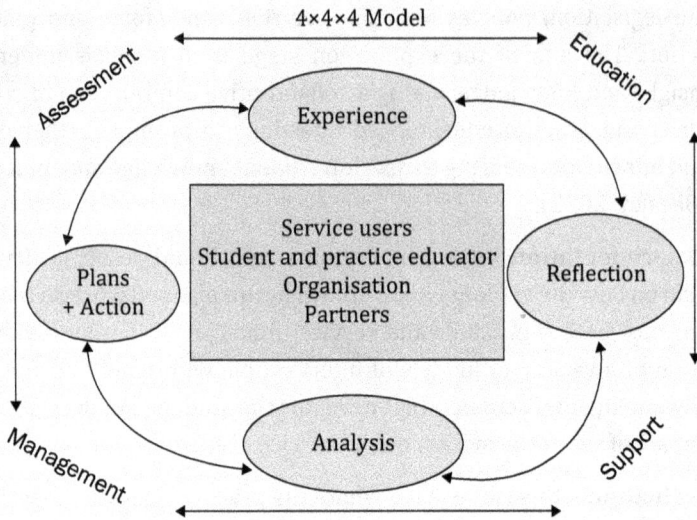

Figure 5.2 4×4×4 Integrated model of supervision (adapted from Morrison, 2005)

The model was developed for qualified social workers: it is explained below and adapted to address supervision within a student placement.

» **The four stakeholders in supervision:** the four stakeholders are at the centre of supervision and their needs and priorities are always kept in mind. They include the service user, supervision participants (student and practice educator), the placement-setting organisation and other partners in the process (these will include external agencies in interprofessional working, university, assessment criteria).

» **The four elements of the supervisory cycle:** based upon experiential learning (Kolb, 1984), the *'reflective supervision cycle'* requires the student and practice educator to *'tell the story'*; reflect on what went well and areas for development; analyse and understand, including application of theory; and identify further goals and plans in order to develop the student's knowledge, skills and values.

» **The four functions of supervision:** these are the functions previously discussed: education, support, management and assessment.

The philosophy behind the model is integrative, where the practice educator and student should consider all areas of the model as they discuss the different issues on the agenda.

Student **development exercise**

Using the 4×4×4 model in Figure 5.2, ask the student to consider a piece of work that they have recently completed.

» First ask the student to consider who the stakeholders are and then consider each one's perspective in turn. Are the needs different dependent on the stakeholder? Are they competing? How does the student balance these needs?

» Next ask the student to reflect upon the undertaken intervention. What can they see worked well, and why might that be? What areas did they find difficult? Ask them to reflect on why that might be and what understanding could they apply to develop greater knowledge, skills and values?

Once the student has completed this exercise, the practice educator should consider if they have utilised each of the four ESMA (Doel, 2010) functions to develop the student's knowledge and skills. If not, consider this as a *'professional development prompt'* to reflect on how they can ensure that they incorporate each of the functions to meet the student's developmental needs.

Finally, while these models are featured in this chapter, it is important to note that other models of supervision exist. One of note is the task-centred model for educational supervision (TCS) (Caspi and Reid, 2002), which offers a strong structure for supervisors and supervisees to follow within and between supervision to develop the supervisee's knowledge, skills and values, particularly where there are areas for development in relation to engaging with set activities. Irrespective of the supervision model used, there is a core supervision process that should be followed within social work student supervision.

Supervision processes

Social work student supervision should involve a number of processes for it to be able to function effectively and efficiently. This section considers the different practical aspects that need to be undertaken by the practice educator, including the supervision agreement, confidentiality, supervision structure and supervision minutes. However, the section begins with a discussion about the supervision life cycle.

Impact **of the pandemic**

Social work student supervision is traditionally undertaken in a quiet room in the placement location. However, where post-pandemic blended placements occur, there may be a need for supervision to be undertaken remotely. All the points covered in this chapter can apply equally to remote supervision. However, it is important that both student and practice educator be committed to logging into the meeting on time and using the video function to maximise the impact of supervision on learning and development (Beesley and Taplin, 2023).

The social work student supervision life cycle

The nature of supervision changes as the placement progresses: expectations shift as the student develops knowledge, skills and confidence. As discussed above, one of the functions of social work student supervision is to facilitate assessment of the student, which includes the formative assessment of the student's knowledge, skills, values and learning needs to ensure that the supervision meets the student's learning needs. It is important that the practice educator constantly adjusts supervision to reflect the student's growing ability and confidence, so that the student is always nurtured and challenged to best develop their knowledge and skills. The social work student supervision life cycle is loosely based on Hawkins and Shohet's (1989) stages of development model.

At the start of the placement, social work student supervision is very much based on relationship building and information sharing. During this stage of the supervision life cycle, it is important that the practice educator develops a clear understanding of the student's previous experiences, abilities and areas for development. As discussed below, the MANDELA model (Tedam, 2012) provides an excellent framework for the importance of the student's prior and lived experience. Indeed, research found that where practice educators explored and valued students' individual previous experiences, strengths, learning styles and needs, they nurtured the supervisory relationship through individualised supervision that facilitated the development of students' knowledge and skills (Yeung et al, 2021). Finally, the practice educator provides a robust induction of pertinent information sharing and checking student understanding, and the emphasis here is more often on the practice educator educating the student.

As the placement progresses and the student is allocated a small caseload, even if that involves co-working, the emphasis shifts to a more case management perspective. Initially, it is important here to ensure that the student knows what is expected of them within the work and is able to ask questions to clarify or seek information; the practice educator may continue with the educating role from the first stage of placement. However, as the student undertakes work with service users, they will return to supervision to update the practice educator on the work undertaken and seek advice and support on the next steps. It is here that the emphasis shifts from educating the student to collaborative discussion, as will be discussed later in this chapter. The practice educator will facilitate the student sharing information and ideas, before supplementing this with practice wisdom, theory, legislation and procedural knowledge, and advice. This is important to develop the student's knowledge, skills and values that they will use in practice.

Finally, as the placement continues and the student gains confidence in their caseload and knowledge of social work practice, the practice educator should facilitate the student to take the lead in the supervision discussions, which they should support and develop through the use of open questions to stimulate further reflection on the matter at hand. Social work student supervision remains important, but the focus has now shifted to supporting the development of knowledge, skills and values rather than teaching them.

It is important not to be too prescriptive about when these shifts should occur, and they will often happen subtly and organically. Students have different learning styles and learning needs and will develop confidence and knowledge at a different pace. Nevertheless, if the practice educator is expecting the student to take the lead from the first supervision, they may need to reflect on whether they are supporting them enough at the start and review their expectations of the student. Similarly, if they find themselves still in the early stages of the life cycle at the interim stage of the placement, it will be time to reflect on why they are still teaching the student. This may be because they have a naturally authoritarian or laissez-faire supervisory style, and it is important to reflect on the importance of student-centred supervision that is able to adapt as the student's learning needs change.

Professional **development prompt**

  » What are your expectations of a student in supervision?

  » Do you think that this differs between first- and final-placement students or between students from different training programmes?

It is worth reflecting on your expectations before your student starts, so that you can adjust your supervisory style to ensure that it is both realistic and appropriate. However, it is important to acknowledge that the practice educator may be feeling overwhelmed by the demands of the role, coupled as it often is with a busy caseload, or they may feel inadequately supported in the role within their own supervision. The practice educator may also fear exposing their own real or imagined inadequacies in the role of supervisor and this in itself can cause anxiety as they are in a role of authority and can feel that they need to be knowledgeable. Here, it is important that the practice educator explores these feelings and identifies solutions to ensure that supervision is collaborative and student-centred. As part of the PEPS (BASW, 2022) training, the qualifying practice educator will be allocated a mentor and they are an excellent source of advice and support.

The supervision agreement

While some students will have experienced supervision in their previous working life or on their first placement, some students will not have had experience of supervision before. Indeed, research has found that social work students often had different or unclear expectations of social work student supervision (Yeung et al, 2021; Beesley, 2022). Thus, a shared understanding of the purpose of supervision by both parties is key. The concept of supervision should be introduced at the very beginning of the placement (at the pre-placement planning meeting and during induction).

Student **development exercise**

»   As practice educator, facilitate a discussion in your first supervision with the student that asks:

»   what have been your experiences of supervision?

»   what do you want to get from supervision?

It is helpful to explore previous experiences with the student and explore their thoughts on the role and purpose of supervision. Beyond their previous experiences, good-quality supervision also needs to take into account the student's existing skills and strengths; their learning needs and areas for development; and their learning style. The completion of a supervision agreement at the first supervision session can be used to facilitate a discussion of these issues, to highlight the centrality of super-vision and to underline a shared understanding of the purpose of supervision. It can also set the tone for the supervisory relationship, which is a partnership where collaborative working is central, and the student is expected to be an active participant. A supervision agreement usually involves the following:

> » timing, regularity and location of supervision;
>
> » recording of supervision notes;
>
> » how interruptions/cancellations/rearrangements will be dealt with;
>
> » expectations and professional responsibilities on both sides regarding the role of supervision, content of the sessions, and preparation and planning involved;
>
> » confidentiality and its limits;
>
> » power and authority issues and further recourse/sources of support available to the student.

A sample supervision agreement is provided in Appendix 1. This should be adapted to reflect the practice educator's placement provision and any individual student requirements.

Confidentiality

It is important to remember that confidentiality in relation to both the student and service users applies to any supervisory discussion. It is important to create a safe space for students to share personal and professional issues, while being aware of the limits of confidentiality. Information that they share about interventions forms part of the case management discussion, and this can be shared with the appropriate professionals involved with the case. In supervision discussions, it may be that the student shares information that requires the practice educator to discuss their progress with their mentor and/or the student's tutor. If this is the case, please ensure that you inform the student of your intention to do this. Finally, the student may share personal information with the practice educator that, provisional to it not being a safeguarding issue, should remain confidential. Confidentiality within social work student supervision is clearly an expectation of both the PEPS (BASW, 2022) and the social work Professional Standards (SWE, 2019).

Structure of supervision

Supervision can be a time-consuming event with an often-onerous agenda. If one considers that the student requires all four functions of supervision – education, support, management and assessment – within a reflective framework, then organisation and structure can facilitate effective supervision (Beesley, 2022). An important piece of practice education practice wisdom is to determine a set day and time each week that social work student supervision will occur and ensure it is diarised from the start of the placement. Equally, identify and pre-book an appropriate space for supervision and ensure that there are no disturbances during it. While crises will happen, the student should never wait for more than a week if rescheduling is difficult.

Supervision can be flexible and responsive to the student's learning needs, but research found that students benefited from well-defined supervision boundaries and valued the ability to collaboratively agree the agenda (Miehls et al, 2013). There will be commonly agreed agenda items, but there may also be items that one or the other participant may not have anticipated, for which it is always important to allocate additional time.

The creation of an agenda is often followed by a *check-in*. The check-in is important as it enables the student to provide context of their week on a personal and professional level and facilitates the practice educator to adjust the supervision accordingly when required. Furthermore, the discussion of non-work-orientated items is an important part of the conversation (Beesley et al, 2018) that relaxes the supervision participants. It facilitates the development of the supervisory relationship, which is critical to the success of the development of knowledge and skills in social work student supervision.

The bulk of the social work student supervision is focused on case management reflective discussion, incorporating theoretical consideration, values and ethical dilemmas, and case planning. It is not necessary to cover every case in every supervision, particularly if there is regular informal supervision between formal supervision sessions, but do ensure that all cases are discussed that need to be discussed each time. Supervision is a time for the practice educator to introduce new case allocations and summarise the pertinent facts and required interventions. In addition to this, there may be specific incidents that require reflective discussion, such as an incident in a team meeting or training session the student attended.

Feedback to students is important within social work student supervision, which should be positive and constructive as well as evidence based, as discussed in Chapter 3. Direct observations, as discussed in Chapter 6, provide excellent feedback points, but it is important that students receive regular feedback so that they are aware of their progress and areas for development. It is not acceptable for a student to wait until they have sight of the interim or final report to know how they are progressing.

Finally, each supervision session should end with a summary of the agreed tasks to be undertaken before the next session by both practice educator and student. This time is time well spent to clarify mutual agreement and meaning from the discussion and to work as a memory aid.

Supervision minutes

The old adage *'if it's not written down, it didn't happen'* applies equally to all levels of supervision in social work, and supervision minutes are critically important. While supervision minutes might be seen as a simple reflection of content in order of discussion, many placement providers now have a supervision record pro forma that can be used or adapted for student supervision. It is worth checking the organisation's expectations with the line manager. The practice wisdom on minute taking is to alternate between each supervision participant taking responsibility for them, but that the other participant should take their own bullet point notes as a memory aid. Many social work students have not taken supervision minutes or meeting minutes before, and this is an excellent opportunity to develop those skills. If the practice educator takes the first, and often second, supervision minutes, they are modelling the level of quality that would be expected by the organisation. Generally, supervision minutes require more than bullet points but less than verbatim notes, with the balance being to ensure that they capture the essence of each discussion for future reference. A common practice is to take a laptop into the supervision and record the minutes as the supervision occurs, but it is important to reflect on whether this creates a barrier between practice educator and student.

The minutes should be typed up and distributed to the other participant within the same week to give time for corrections to be made before the next supervision, at which point the record should be signed by both participants. Supervision minutes should be held by both participants and can often be used as evidence of meeting assessment criteria by the student, or as evidence of lack of completion of tasks where there are concerns. Finally, where local practice dictates that supervision decisions about service users are recorded in service user files, it should be made clear who is responsible for this task.

Addressing power in social work student supervision

There is an inherent power differential within the supervisory relationship between practice educator and student, which comes from the assessment function of the role of practice educator.

Professional **development prompt**

Reflect back to supervision that you received as a social work student.

» Was it an empowering experience? What was it that you liked about it? How can you apply that to your own supervisory style?

» Was it a difficult experience? If so, what power dynamics can you identify that may have damaged it? How can you ensure that your supervisory style is authoritative?

This professional development prompt is important as it asks the practice educator to be reflective and become aware of their own identity as a supervisee and supervisor, and in turn to be empathically attuned to the student's responses and individual learning needs and style. Unfortunately, some readers will have identified with the second bullet point, and our hope is that you are now able to use your difficult experience as a learning experience, where you are able to avoid the same pitfalls that your practice educator fell into.

This section reflects on the MANDELA model, and the impact that the supervisory relationship and collaborative supervision can have on reducing the power imbalance.

MANDELA model (Tedam, 2012)

Research has identified that student-centred practice education that entails the practice educator understanding the student is productive in enabling the development of the student's knowledge and skills (Beesley, 2022). One model that may be helpful for practice educators in developing an understanding of their student is the MANDELA model (Tedam, 2012). This was developed in response to the particular issues faced by students of Black African heritage studying on social work courses at Tedam's university, where such students were more likely to fail practice placements than white students. This pattern is duplicated in other universities, where Black African students or other Black or Asian students are overly represented in failed placements. The MANDELA model can be used by practice educators and students to understand and appreciate the differences and similarities of life experience that a student brings to the placement; in addition:

it models best practice in that it provides an open, honest and reflective forum in which discussions about experiences, needs and differences can be examined, respected and understood.

(Tedam, 2012, p 68)

The MANDELA model asks the practice educator to **M**ake time for the student and **A**cknowledge their individual **N**eeds, **D**ifferences, **E**ducational experiences, **L**ife experiences and **A**ge. Firstly, the model advises that students have different learning needs and styles and they will develop their knowledge and skills at a different pace. Furthermore, while a student may intuitively develop one skill, they may need more support or time with another. Time spent understanding the student and adjusting your practice educator style will enhance the development of the student's knowledge and skills (Beesley, 2022).

Issues of difference and similarity should be explicitly explored. Here it is important to reflect that similarities in identity do not automatically equate to similarities in values, learning styles or lived experiences, and that the practice educator should listen to the student's perspective at all times. While the model initially focuses on ethnic or cultural similarities or differences, issues of gender, age, sexuality, etc should also be considered. Indeed, within African contexts, age is an important variable in understanding relationships and interactions, as is the role of *'teacher'*, and expectations should be discussed in induction to avoid barriers to learning. Finally, identity differences can lead to exasperated power differentials, and it is important that the practice educator takes account of how the student is feeling and makes adjustments in order to maximise ability to engage with learning opportunities.

The model then considers the individual student and reflects on the importance of understanding any particular needs and how to address these needs collaboratively with the student, such as English language proficiency skills, general communication skills or written skills. It is worth noting that most employers and universities will have access to advice and support for students where English is not their first language. It is important that the practice educator recognises the importance and potential impact of educational and life experiences, as bad educational experiences or individual or institutional oppression can deter a student from engaging with a well-meaning practice educator. Finally, and returning to one of Knowles' (1973) andragogical principles, it is important for the practice educator to explore, respect and build upon the student's life and work experiences to ensure learning is appropriate and student-centred.

Case **example**

Hope is a Black African student on her first placement in a voluntary agency. She is given constructive feedback, using the SCORE model outlined in Chapter 3, that she lacks empathy when she talks to service users. Hope becomes quiet and withdrawn on receiving the feedback and rings in sick for the remainder of the week. On her return to placement the following week, the white male practice educator asks Hope if she is okay, but she seems reluctant to discuss how she feels. However, the practice educator persists and outlines to Hope the importance of constructive feedback and that he views it as a starting point to develop the skills of empathy and that he has lots of ideas to support her in this.

Hope explains that she has experienced feedback on a previous course which was highly negative and not constructive, and that she was expecting the feedback to mean she will fail the placement. Once she begins reflecting, she shares that she is finding it difficult to ask for help from a younger white man as she is expecting him to judge her as a 'silly old Black woman' given her past experiences in a social care role have been that her views have been dismissed.

» Using the MANDELA model, can you identify how the practice educator could:

Make time for the student and Acknowledge their individual Needs, Differences, Educational experiences, Life experiences and Age?

This case example illustrates how despite providing feedback using evidence-based good practice, the practice educator has come from a position of white privilege to assume that Hope would be able to hear and accept the constructive feedback. However, when he returns to the basics of explaining the role of feedback, he is able to identify that Hope's self-confidence has been eroded by her educational and life experiences so she has different needs in receiving feedback than he would. It may be helpful to reflect that following Hope's disclosure, the practice educator was able to provide feedback in a way that emphasised it as a collaborative learning activity. Furthermore, he reflected that had he used the MANDELA model with Hope prior to giving the feedback, he could have avoided Hope becoming upset and missing placement days. Hope went on to pass her placement successfully.

Tedam (2012) quite correctly argues that it is only through understanding the individual student's learning needs that the practice educator can ensure that the student is empowered to engage with learning on placement. A final word on the MANDELA model is that while it was developed for practice educators working with students of Black African heritage, it can be applied as an excellent model to ensure student-centred learning for all students.

The supervisory relationship

In order to reduce the power differential, the supervisory relationship is considered key (Roulston et al, 2018; Ketner et al, 2017; Yeung et al, 2021; Beesley, 2022). Research has identified that a weak supervisory relationship can exacerbate a stressful situation and if a student is struggling to develop knowledge or a skill, they will only ask for support if there is a strong relationship (Litvack et al, 2010). It is here that the nurturing of a safe and supportive supervisory relationship is critical to avoid such downward and counter-productive cycles of detrimental supervision. Indeed, Ingram (2015) recognised that an *emotionally inclusive supervisory relationship* enables supervisees to discuss the emotional aspects of practice. By contrast he identified that in supervision where the supervisee felt that procedural case management discussions took priority, there was reduced space for reflection and exploration of emotional responses. It is the practice educator's responsibility to nurture the supervisory relationship so that the student feels safe to explore their ideas and emotions. In so doing, they can engage in the reflective discussion that we identified earlier in this chapter as contributing to the development of knowledge and skills.

Professional **development prompt**

Consider how the supervisory relationship will be influenced by your own experiences of supervision as a supervisee.

» If you have had poor supervision, how did that impact your engagement with supervision?

» If you have experienced supervision that you felt worked well, consider what aspects of it were beneficial.

» Consider and list some of the differences between supervision you experienced as a student and as an employee.

By giving thought to this, and acknowledging these influences, you will begin to develop a sense of the style of supervisor you would like to be or wish to avoid becoming. This reflective approach is an important part of your development as a practice educator because being aware of your favoured style will enable you to use it well; and as you develop a relationship with your student, you will be able to adapt it to meet their learning needs and learning style.

In her doctoral research, Beesley (2022) found that student research participants valued a collaborative supervisory relationship, which they identified as being created through a feeling of being comfortable, open and honest; this mirrored previous research into social work student supervision by Lefevre (2005). This enabled student research participants to ask questions and offer different perspectives to explore their understanding and develop their knowledge and skills. Practice educator research participants viewed a collaborative supervisory relationship as a friendly and approachable style, with well-defined supervision boundaries, aligning with research by Litvack et al (2010) and Miehls et al (2013). Finally, Beesley identified that a collaborative supervisory relationship was *'warm'*, *'friendly'*, *'open'* included *'humour'*, was *'enthusiastic'*, *'valuing'* and involved *'showing interest'* with professional boundaries applied.

It is interesting to note that many of the characteristics and skills that a practice educator requires are ones that are developed as a social worker. The social worker needs good communication skills (Beesley et al, 2018), as does the practice educator. The social worker is required to be aware of power, authority and oppression (Tedam, 2021), as does the practice educator. The social worker empowers the service user to enhance their skills for a clear outcome (Adams, 2008), as does the practice educator. However, there is a subtle difference in the supervisory relationship, as it is one that is arguably more intense than the social worker/service user one because the practice educator is often located within the same office or team and the relationship is based on a work-related dynamic as colleagues, albeit with a hierarchical foundation.

Finally, while social work is often undertaken individually with service users, the team observe the supervisory relationship outside supervision and may contribute thoughts, feelings and opinions that can impact the supervisory relationship both positively and negatively. A student who engages with practice educators, the placement team, service users and other professionals alike is a joy, or it may be that the practice educator and student 'click' and have a naturally easy supervisory relationship. However, as will be discussed in Chapter 7, where a student is struggling on placement, it can impact the practice educator, the supervisory relationship and the team, yet the practice educator must continue to strive to create a collaborative supervisory relationship to support the student's development of knowledge and skills. Irrespective, a nuanced student-centred approach, where the practice educator is flexible and responsive to students' individual needs, is considered the most appropriate practice educator style (Gardiner, 1988; Beesley, 2022).

Collaboration

Collaboration is more than one participant working in partnership to enhance outcomes (Whittington, 2003). When related to social work student supervision, collaboration involves the participation of both practice educator and student. Indeed, research has found that supervision should be undertaken *together* to facilitate the student's development of their knowledge and skills and the importance of both participants being able to express their perspective to explore a situation (Brodie and Williams, 2013; Beesley, 2022). This sits within a student-centred approach, based on many of the Rogerian (1967) principles of person-centred practice. In student-centred supervision, the student is the central focus of the supervision, is involved in all decision making about themselves and has their learning needs met.

A collaborative approach can be taken throughout social work student supervision, starting with the mutual agreement of the agenda to ensure that the student's requirements are allocated both time and attention. It is important in discussion that the practice educator is supportive and enables the student to set out their perspective first. This can be stimulated by open questions by the practice educator that stimulate further reflective discussion and information sharing of theory, practice wisdom, and procedural and legislative requirements by the practice educator to develop knowledge and skills. Finally, it is important to remember to be non-judgemental in your responses to the student's perspective. The concept that there is *no such thing as a bad idea* lends itself to seeing all student ideas as a starting point for a reflective discussion about why they think that way and to explore other viewpoints to enhance understanding and knowledge.

Case **example**

You are in a supervision session with Isla, a student who is midway through her final 100-day placement in a statutory children and families team. She has been to visit the Sykes family following an incident where their 14-year-old daughter Lauren recently left the family home after an argument and is now staying with a friend, refusing to return. Isla visited Lauren in school and Lauren had told her that there had been a family argument about her being rude and staying out late, and she had walked out in response. She had stayed two nights at a friend's house and was refusing to return home, although not giving many reasons other than saying her parents were always shouting at her and that she had had enough. Isla has just been to visit Lauren's parents, Mr and Mrs Sykes. In response to your enquiry about how the visit went, Isla replies:

'The visit was just awful! Mr and Mrs Sykes were there and also Lauren's gran, Mrs Ayre, although she doesn't live with them; but she did most of the talking. I was trying to ask Mr and Mrs Sykes what the argument with Lauren had been about as I hadn't got much detail from Lauren, just that she was adamant she wasn't going to return home. To be honest, she was quite sullen when I was trying to talk to her. The grandmother, Mrs Ayre, started shouting that Lauren was no good, ungrateful and cheeky, and that her son had a weak heart and health problems, and he wasn't even Lauren's real dad anyway. I was just sitting in the middle of it all. There didn't seem to be anything I could say or do that wouldn't make the situation worse. Mr Sykes then stood up and said he had had enough of all the problems this was causing and he left the room and then Mrs Ayre stormed out saying that I was just wasting time and that Lauren should stay where she was. I just feel I didn't get very far with either of them... I feel awful about it; it was just a mess!

'But once they had both left, Mrs Sykes calmed down. It was so much better then! I was able to talk to her and listen to what she wanted. She feels that Mr Sykes and Lauren are constantly arguing, and she feels stuck in the middle of it. She is happy for Lauren to stay with her friend for another couple of days and she knows the mum well. After chatting, we agreed that she would give Lauren a ring when Mr Sykes was at his mum's house and make sure that she was okay. I said I'd call back in a day or two. Is that okay?'

» What questions could you ask Isla to support her to reflect on this intervention, using any of the models from this chapter?

» What knowledge might you need to share with Isla to develop her understanding of complex relationship dynamics?

» What questions could you ask to stimulate an empathic discussion about why Lauren was *'sullen'* in their meeting?

» What positives can you give to Isla from her description?

» What areas for development might you want to raise with her?

» What questions can you ask the student to support their formulation of a plan to engage the service user moving forward?

This is not an unusual social work student supervision discussion. It is clear that Isla felt overwhelmed by the family dynamics, and it will be important to ensure that she receives praise from you that she had the resilience to remain in the house, and that she was able to engage Mrs Sykes once it was quieter and left with a plan in place to move the situation forward. However, it also appears that Isla needs support developing how she deals with conflict, and this may be an area for development within your next supervision session. A good way to approach this is to ask if she would like to address developing confidence in dealing with conflict as an area for development, and to attend supervision with prepared ideas and activities to support Isla. In addition, you should offer Isla support in relation to how she is impacted by the conflict within the family, ensuring that she is debriefed from it and is not taking stress from the visit home with her. Furthermore, it will be important in supervision to facilitate a reflective discussion on Isla's values in relation to the family and how this impacted her interventions; some of the student development exercises in Chapter 4 could be helpful here.

The important element here is a collaborative approach to the reflective learning model (Davys and Beddoe, 2009). It is important to remember that supervision should be a *dialogue* and that these questions and prompts can be used as tools to *encourage student engagement* in the supervision session and not as either an 'inquisition' or a question/answer session. If the practice educator feels supervision is turning into the latter, with them continually posing questions and the student giving limited answers, then they need to acknowledge, discuss and address this with the student. It would be helpful to revisit the supervision agreement and supervision expectations with the student and reiterate the expectations regarding collaborative working and the student's contribution to supervision. However, remember to ask the student *why* they answer with brevity, thus engaging them collaboratively.

Conclusion

This chapter has considered the role of the practice educator in providing effective social work student supervision. Different models of supervision have been suggested and the processes of supervision throughout the placement have been examined. Collaborative supervision and the supervisory relationship have been discussed as a means of reducing the inherent power differential, together with the necessity for practice educators to embrace a continuing awareness of the impact of these differentials within supervision.

As the chapter ends, it is appropriate to revisit the purpose of social work student supervision as the site of the development of knowledge, skills and values from experiential learning through collaborative reflective discussion. Research has identified that practice educators view social work student supervision as beneficial to both their own development and the development of students' knowledge and skills (Ketner et al, 2017), while it is valued by students because it develops their skills (Wilson and Flanagan, 2021). This reminds us that while students may not be keen on theory, it is our duty as practice educators that we provide reflective and collaborative social work student supervision that develops students' knowledge, skills and values.

Taking it further

Kadushin, A and Harkness, D (2014) *Supervision in Social Work.* New York: Columbia University Press. The fifth edition of Kadushin's (1976) functional model of social work supervision provides a robust discussion of the first three functions (education, support and management).

Morrison, T (2005) *Staff Supervision in Social Care.* Brighton: Pavillion. This book has stood the test of time to offer accessible and practical advice on how to provide supervision effectively.

Wonnacott, J (2012) *Mastering Social Work Supervision.* London: Jessica Kingsley. A text written for social work supervisors that clearly explains the link between effective supervision and effective outcomes for service users.

Chapter aims

» To establish core principles of fair assessment.

» To understand the different stages of assessment within social work placement.

» To explore collaborative assessment.

Critical **questions**

» How do you maintain the role of assessor and supporter/educator of the student?

» How do you ensure that assessment decisions are the outcomes of informed, evidence-based judgements?

» How do you involve the student, service user and colleagues in the assessment process?

Introduction

This chapter aligns with the Practice Educator Professional Standards for social work (PEPS) (BASW, 2022) Domain C '*manage the fair and transparent assessment of students in practice*' and the statement of values. The critical questions develop your ability to meet these requirements and will be supported through the chapter. Assessment of a social work student is a complex activity, and it is the responsibility of the practice educator to determine if the student has successfully completed and passed their placement. The assessment role can be extremely anxiety provoking, requiring judgement about a student as to their suitability and capability for their own profession.

This chapter will guide the reader to an understanding of the practice educator's role as assessor of the student on social work placement. It will begin with an introduction to the concept of assessment itself, and outline the notion of diagnostic, formative and summative assessment; relevant, valid, reliable and sufficient assessment; triangulation; cognitive bias; and culturally sensitive assessment. It will consider assessment criteria, which include both the Professional Capabilities Framework (PCF) domains (BASW, 2018) and individual learning outcomes, before reflecting on the specific assessment of students on the social work placement, which includes informal assessment, supervision, direct observations, assessment of social work values and academic work. It will provide advice on assessment to inform the interim and final reports. The chapter concludes with discussion centred on collaborative assessment.

Assessment

Assessment can be argued to be the task of ascertaining whether or not a student has met the expected criteria to enable them to progress. It requires determination of whether or not there has been sufficient development of identified knowledge and skills to enable students to pass their placement. However, assessment is much more complex than that. A wider task-definition of assessment beyond the final outcome is expanded to include the determination of what students know and the ongoing task of student education (Williams and Rutter, 2021). It is this purpose that will be applied to this chapter, where assessment will be seen as both a pinpoint of the student's knowledge and skills at the end of placement, and as an ongoing task throughout placement that facilitates feedback and informs the development of their knowledge, skills and values.

This section reflects on diagnostic, formative and summative assessment; relevant, valid, reliable and sufficient assessment; triangulation; cognitive bias; and culturally sensitive assessment.

Diagnostic, formative and summative assessment

Doel's (2010) functions of social work supervision embody the roles of the practice educator as required to Educate, Support, Manage and Assess students. These should not be seen as separate functions, but as each one in turn informing the next. Nevertheless, these functions highlight a role conflict that can potentially create practice educator anxiety, where the need to educate and support the student to enable knowledge and skill development may be considered to be in direct contrast to the need to assess the student. It is hoped that this chapter will support the practice educator's understanding of the integration of learning and assessment.

The notion of different forms of assessment comes from Black (1993) but has since been further developed. Explicitly incorporating the notion of diagnostic, formative and summative assessment into practice learning may help avoid confusion and anxiety for a student and help define and develop the practice educator's roles of support, education and assessment.

»   **Diagnostic assessment:** intended to identify existing strengths, learning needs and the types of teaching and learning strategies needed to suit the learner's style. This is often undertaken most robustly during induction or when a new skill is introduced to the student. This is an informal assessment developed through collaborative discussion with the student in supervision and in less formal relationship-developing discussions. It enables the practice educator to ensure that the support and teaching of the student is student-centred and appropriate to meeting their individual learning needs.

»   **Formative assessment:** intended to enable the learner to assimilate feedback in order to progress their learning. It is an assessment of the student's development of knowledge and skills thus far to enable identification of strengths to build upon and areas for continued development. This means that it provides positive and constructive feedback, as discussed in Chapter 3. It enables the student to know what they need to do to succeed in both knowledge and skill development and in passing the placement. However, formative feedback can also operate to improve the teaching and support that the practice educator provides, utilising the same ideas of diagnostic assessment.

»   **Summative assessment:** intended as the final assessment against the agreed learning outcomes and external criteria following a set period, normally a module, topic or term's teaching. Within social work placement, this translates as the practice educator's final assessment of '*pass*' or '*fail*' which is made at the end of the placement. The summative assessment enables the assessor to summarise the student's development and provide feedforward for future areas for development. This is often based on a social work placement portfolio or collaborative discussion with the student of evidence of their capability and development within each of the nine PCF domains (BASW, 2018), as well as the formative assessment that has been undertaken throughout the placement.

In order to maximise the value of diagnostic and formative assessment, it is important to plan and create opportunities to enable the student to learn from feedback and follow up on subsequent learning needs, which in turn contributes to the summative assessment.

Case **example**

An initial discussion at the practice learning agreement meeting for a first placement in an organisation offering support for carers identified that the student (Sophia) had no previous experience of carrying out assessments and this was consequently highlighted as one of her learning needs. In supervision, the diagnostic assessment *was undertaken through a reflective discussion that identified an analysis of the knowledge and skills that would be needed for the task, which was supplemented with a list of areas where Sophia needed to develop her practice in order to offer an effective intervention. Relevant research, teaching and rehearsal then took place to develop Sophia's transferable knowledge and skills and to address gaps.*

A direct observation was planned as a formative assessment *of the student's learning. It was observed as a result that Sophia had good communication skills but did not have enough knowledge of the eligibility criteria for the respite service, so she was asked to research these criteria and present them in the next supervision session. A further discussion confirmed that this knowledge was embedded, and this piece of work could then contribute to the* summative assessment *of Sophia's capability across several PCF domains.*

» Reflect on each of the assessment stages and how they are applied with Sophia.

» Now reflect on your own practice with your student: can you identify when you are applying each different assessment type?

It is helpful to be clear in your understanding of the different assessment types as confusing the summative assessment with the formative assessment may, for example, result in a premature final assessment that is either generous or unfair, and certainly does not reflect the student's final stage of development.

Relevant, valid, reliable and sufficient assessment

The PCF (BASW, 2018) provides a clear standard of practice that practice educators must assess a social work student against in order to complete their summative assessment. However, that is often subject to personal interpretation and professional judgement. Irrespective of the outcome of the practice educator's summative assessment, they are required to justify their decision both to the student and to external bodies. This means that, like providing feedback, the summative assessment must be evidence based, providing examples of work undertaken by the student to support the judgement. The following principles are intended to help the practice educator make sure that the evidence upon which they base their decision is rigorous and underpinned by fairness.

» **Relevance:** choose an appropriate method of assessment to measure the task, knowledge or skill being assessed.

The practice educator could have assessed Sophia's written skills by reading the initial assessment; however, a discussion would enable assessment of critical analysis and decision-making skills that informed the assessment outcome. Furthermore, the direct observation facilitated assessment of the student's communication skills. Here we see that understanding what is to be assessed is critical in informing how to assess.

» **Validity:** ensure that the evidence demonstrates what it is intended to test and enables the student to demonstrate the agreed objective.

In the case study, the practice educator identified that it was Sophia's ability to undertake assessments that was the identified learning need. Had the direct observation been undertaken in the following home visit where Sophia provided feedback on the outcome of the initial assessment, it is unlikely that the student's ability to assess the service user would have been evident. Here we see the importance of good planning and communication with the student.

» **Reliability and sufficiency:** observe a good breadth and number of interventions in order to establish that the student's knowledge and skills are consistently applied.

If the practice educator undertook all three direct observations of Sophia carrying out initial assessments, while this would enable assessment of the development of her ability to carry out initial assessments, it would limit the breadth of evidence that the practice educator was able to gather. Here we see that the practice educator should undertake diagnostic and formative assessment frequently through the placement, and not limit observation of practice to the direct observation points in order to build a consistent picture of the student's knowledge and skills.

The concepts of relevance, validity, reliability and sufficiency are important ones to bear in mind as diagnostic, formative and summative assessment of the student is undertaken.

Professional **development prompt**

> » Take one of your student's learning objectives and your assessment of their progress in that area. Reflect how you have applied each of the principles above. This is designed to make you think about *how* you assess your student and ensure it remains objective and fair.

Triangulation

One way of ensuring fairness is to use a variety of assessment methods, enabling a triangulation of evidence (Shardlow and Doel, 1993). Indeed, this will ensure that the principles of fair assessment (relevance, validity, reliability and sufficiency) are applied across the breadth of assessment strategies. Triangulation can involve the use of a range of assessment methods, which will increase the reliability of the summative assessment as students display different strengths and areas for development in different assessment situations. There are many ways to assess a student, including:

» direct observation of practice;

» co-working a case;

» request feedback from colleagues and other involved professionals;

» request feedback from service users;

» read case notes and reports;

» supervision discussion;

» read reflective accounts;

» read academic work based on placement learning;

» evidence in evidence portfolio/grid.

The practice educator should incorporate each of these different strategies to ensure a holistic and reliable assessment of the student's knowledge and skills. Some of these assessment strategies will be discussed later in this chapter.

Triangulation of assessment can also occur through the use of multiple assessors. The practice educator remains the lead assessor and is responsible for the final summative assessment in relation to the placement but gathering the views of other invested parties can enhance objectivity (Williams and Rutter, 2021). These can be people with different roles such as service users, colleagues and allied professionals. Their different perspectives on the same piece of work can inform a rounded assessment of the process, as they may offer different perspectives. A systematic and transparent approach to this is needed, so that the student's development is noted and analysed, the contributions of each participant are meaningful, and appropriate feedback and support is given to the student as part of ongoing developmental supervision.

Cognitive bias

In making any decision or judgement we rely on information that we have available to us, which includes an objective and a subjective perspective. The objective perspective is where evidence of the facts in front of us is used to make a decision. However, the analysis of the observation of practice may in itself be dependent on a subjective assessment or cognitive bias (Tversky and Kahneman, 1974), and an awareness of this is very important for the practice educator. Cognitive biases may occur in the following forms.

Confirmation bias: where the practice educator may become attached to one view of the student. This may have been formed early in the relationship or placement and may quickly become a self-fulfilling prophecy as the practice educator may become unable to see or accept any evidence that counters her original or underlying judgement. While this may benefit the student where the bias is that they are a *'great'* student, it can be highly detrimental when the practice educator determines that they are incapable and therefore are unable to identify any development of knowledge and skills irrespective of ability.

Heuristic bias: where previous examples come to mind and comparisons and assumptions are made. A student may be judged relatively to another, previous, or even current, student, and the true frequency of their behaviour may be exaggerated because of the recollection of the previous student. Alternatively, the student may be judged as inferior to a previous exceptional student. Finally, this can happen when the practice educator takes a first-placement student after a final-placement student and expects equal knowledge and skills.

Attribution bias: where the practice educator attributes, expects and sees certain traits in the student due to their identity. This judgemental approach is dangerous and against social work values. How to support students from a Black and global minority heritage is addressed in Chapter 3.

Bandwagon effect bias: where the practice educator accedes to the dominant judgement of the student within the workplace or team, be that positive or negative, and often based on different assessment criteria. The practice educator may then be unable to express or even form alternative views of the student.

Egocentric bias: where the practice educator is unable to hear anyone's perspective but their own.

Risk aversion: where the practice educator is cautious in their assessment of the student and where the assessment is borderline fails the student rather than providing additional support to help them pass the placement.

Decision avoidance: where given the time-consuming and emotionally challenging nature of taking action, particularly where a student may be causing concern, decisions that are likely to invoke some action may be avoided.

Each of these cognitive biases can result in a subjective assessment, often without the practice educator being aware of it, and can be highly detrimental to the student. Even where they are the benefactor of a positive cognitive bias in the formative assessment, it may limit the learning opportunities that are offered due to an assumption of existing knowledge and skills. However, in many more situations it limits the expectations on the student's learning opportunities and stunts the development of knowledge and skills. It is critical here that the practice educator is aware of the impact of self on the student (Beesley, 2022), thus enhancing both access to learning opportunities and a fair assessment. This can be achieved through reflection on practice as well as discussion with a practice educator mentor.

Culturally sensitive assessment

Every student should receive a fair assessment, and this chapter's aim is to provide support and guidance to the practice educator to ensure that occurs. Nevertheless, the practice educator should be sensitive to and aware of the cultural needs of students when assessing them. Throughout this book there have been discussions about meeting the learning needs of students from a Black and global minority heritage or who have additional learning needs due to a disability. Indeed, suggestions have been offered on how to attend to these issues to maximise engagement in learning activities and to promote the development of knowledge, skills and values. The practice educator's role is to support the student to be equipped to successfully navigate the stages of diagnostic, formative and summative assessment.

However, it is noteworthy that even in the assessment stage practice educators should be aware of supporting students non-judgementally. Cultural awareness is important, but simply asking the student about their individual cultural customs enhances this and can reduce the negative impact of assessment assumptions. For example, where the student is fasting through the daytime, a late afternoon assessment may be detrimental to the outcome as their focus may be waning, but this cannot be assumed. Furthermore, understanding of cultural norms may explain the student's behaviours; for example, what the student sees as a deference to the practice educator as the *'teacher'* may be interpreted by the practice educator as disinterest, poor motivation or lack of understanding, but this can be addressed and resolved in collaborative reflective discussion.

Social workers will argue that social work values mean that they treat everyone equally, yet proportionally more students from a Black and global minority heritage fail their placement (Fairtlough et al, 2014). It is important here to be aware of cognitive bias, racism and ableism when assessing a student, and to ensure that critical reflexivity is applied, which can be enhanced through discussion with a practice educator mentor.

Assessment criteria

Social work students are subject to assessment through a number of different assessment criteria, including the PCF (BASW, 2018), the Knowledge and Skills Statements (KSS) (DoH, 2015; DfE, 2018) and for those students undertaking a social work apprenticeship, the Knowledge, Skills and Behaviours (KSBs) (IATE, 2018). However, for the purpose of this chapter the PCF (BASW, 2018) will be assumed to be the primary assessment criteria. This section considers development and assessment against the individually identified learning outcomes.

Professional Capabilities Framework (BASW, 2018)

The PCF (BASW, 2018) is a holistic assessment that requires social work students and social workers to develop their skills throughout their professional career with nine domains, as illustrated in Figure 6.1.

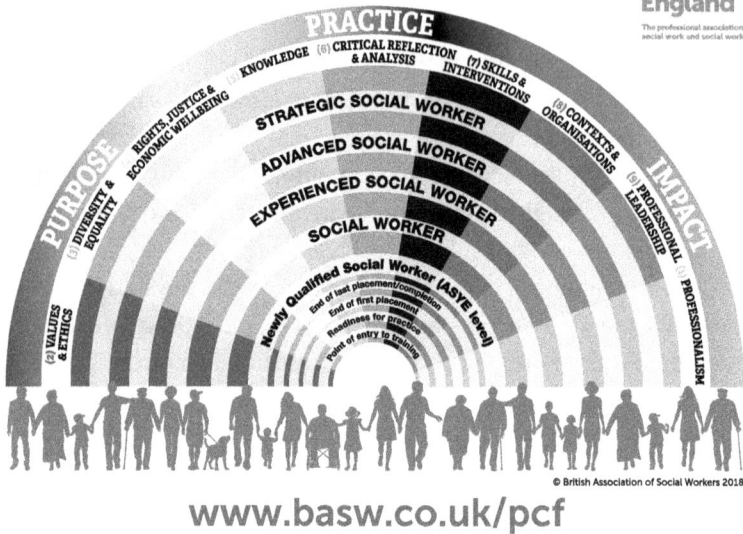

Figure 6.1 PCF fan graphic (BASW, 2018)

The PCF is based upon *development* in each domain. This is important, as it requires that as each level is met, a minimum level of competence must be demonstrated, but also that progression must be made in each area. This means that even the skilled social work student must develop knowledge and skills in all domains within the placement. Furthermore, the emphasis on passing all nine domains means that students who are strong in one domain cannot ignore another domain; for example, a strong practical student cannot not apply theory to their practice. This ensures that students are holistic learners. Indeed, in order to assess *competence*, the practice educator merely needs to see evidence of a completed task, whereas when assessing *capability* (the potential to do something), the practice educator is required to assess both the student's skill base and, crucially, their thinking. In preparation for placement, the practice educator should familiarise themselves with the level required for the student, and review this at interim and final report writing stages.

Professional **development prompt**

» Reflect on what you consider good enough practice in each domain, and how a student could demonstrate it within your placement setting.

» Reflect if there is practice in each domain that would be an indicator that the student had areas for development.

PCF domain	Good practice	Practice that would raise concern
1. Professionalism		
2. Values		
3. Diversity		
4. Rights		
5. Knowledge		
6. Critical analysis and reflection		
7. Intervention and skills		
8. Contexts and organisations		
9. Professional leadership		

Figure 6.2 PCF assessment grid

By completing Figure 6.2, you are being asked to reflect on your expectations of a student within your placement. Firstly, when considering your expectations of the student it is helpful to think about what you will view as good-enough practice. Each practice educator will interpret the PCF guidance (BASW, 2018) slightly differently, as our expectations for students will vary slightly. However, this professional development prompt enables you to develop a sense of identity as a practice educator and your personal assessment criteria.

Learning outcomes

As part of academic learning at university, students are familiar with the notion of learning outcomes and objectives and with the alignment of teaching and assessment methods with learning outcomes. Practice learning should be no different; students should have a clear set of objectives to meet. The student's learning needs are often supplied to the practice educator in the placement application form (PAF) and elaborated upon in the placement learning agreement (PLA) meeting and induction. These should be updated throughout the placement and may include areas for development identified during formative assessment. The practice educator should ensure that the learning outcomes are clear, that appropriate support and teaching is provided, and that appropriate learning opportunities are provided to enable the student to develop and demonstrate the knowledge and skills identified in the learning need.

The PCF promotes a progressive approach, inviting the practice educator to make explicit the student's progress throughout the placement, and helping the student to understand their development in the context of their overall education and career pathway. All elements of the assessment should contribute to the summative assessment, including areas of relative weakness or uncertain development. As stated, the process of the placement should become more important than the outcome.

Assessment in the social work placement

Stone (2018) identified that social work students often do not know how or when they will be assessed, which is a fundamental requirement of valuing the student. It is imperative that the practice educator facilitates open, honest and clear discussions with the student about all assessment areas in the social work placement. Indeed, Stone (2018) recommends that the Transparency of Assessment in Practice Education (TAPE) model of assessment is applied to all forms of assessment of students on social work placement. This involves ensuring that the student knows and understands what she refers as the 6Ws.

> » *Who* will be undertaking the assessment? – be that a named person or an identified collective.

> » *When* will the assessment occur? – be that at a specific time or an ongoing assessment.

> » *Why* is the assessment required? – ensuring that it meets the named assessment criteria and is relevant, valid, reliable and sufficient.

> » *Where* will the assessment occur? – including physical spaces such as the team room or the service user's house and intangible spaces including supervision.

> » *Way* – this reflects on how the assessment will be undertaken.

> » *What* will the assessment assess? – against clear learning objectives.

The TAPE model of assessment values the student and ensures that they are informed of the ongoing outcome of the assessment while they are on placement. This section reflects on the specific assessment of students on the social work placement, which includes informal assessment, supervision, direct observations, assessment of social work values and academic work. It will provide advice on assessment to inform the interim and final reports.

Ongoing informal assessment

While the rest of this section reflects on specific points where assessment may be considered more specifically, it is important to first note that the assessment of the student by the practice educator should be ongoing throughout the placement. This is not to say, to quote from the *Monsters Inc* movie, that you should be '*always watching*', but to remind the practice educator, and indeed the student, that the student is being assessed throughout each and every day of their placement. This means that, for example, should a student think that racist jokes while making coffee are acceptable, then this would raise concerns about both their professionalism and values. In turn, these would inform the formative assessment and stimulate directed support on social work values, as well as highlighting the importance of anti-discriminatory and anti-oppressive practice. However, informal assessment also includes the student's knowledge and skill development in day-to-day tasks and interventions, which will be undertaken by the practice educator through informal observation of practice through co-working and accessing reports and case recordings, etc.

Social work student supervision provides a further form of informal assessment. As discussed in Chapter 5, it provides the functions of education, support, management and assessment (ESMA) (Doel, 2010), and it is the assessment function that we focus on in this discussion. Supervision enables the practice educator to undertake diagnostic and formative assessment of the student's knowledge and skills, that is, to assess what the student knows, how they apply it to social work interventions through reflective discussion, and to identify the areas to focus on supporting the student to develop.

It is important to be clear with the student about the importance of informal assessment throughout the entirety of the placement in relation to the summative assessment. However, Stone (2018) noted that students found this panoptic approach to be surveillant and oppressive rather than empowering; therefore, it is important that it is discussed and explained in induction and revisited throughout the placement to ensure that students are aware of the ongoing informal assessment and understand its role in diagnostic and formative assessment.

Impact of the pandemic

It can be argued that informal assessment is most impacted by blended location placements. The informal observation of practice and office-based discussions form a critical part of the practice educator's assessment of the student, and the opportunity to do this may be reduced in a blended location placement. As in an office-based placement, the practice educator will need to monitor the student's work to ensure that the work is being done and undertaken and to the required placement standard. Remote or blended location placements may thus require a more rigorous quality assurance strategy, including regular accessing of case records and reports, and additional informal observations of practice, which can be undertaken in person or during remote communication appointments.

It is important for the practice educator to remember that they are skilled at assessing situations and service users with relatively little input and that these are transferable skills, so that the focus shifts to quality over quantity of assessment of the student.

Direct observation of practice

Direct observations of practice are traditionally seen as the most reliable way of gathering evidence of a student's practice, knowledge and skills, and a minimum of three direct observations of the student are required. A minimum of two of these must be undertaken by the practice educator, and it is often good practice to liaise with the student and an appropriate colleague so that this colleague conducts at least one direct observation. It is also good practice to undertake a minimum of one direct observation in the first month of the placement to enable diagnostic assessment, a second direct observation around the interim point, and a third one with a month left of the placement.

Direct observation remains one of the most anxiety-provoking activities for a student. Inevitably, the artificiality of the situation along with the discomfort that it can cause to both student and service user can impact considerably on the performance of the student. Thus, careful planning, implementation and feedback with the student are necessary to maximise the learning that can take place. Many students see the direct observation activity as a pass or fail point. Therefore, time should be spent with them discussing that while the direct observations do indeed inform the summative assessment, they are designed far more as a diagnostic or formative assessment to inform the practice educator of strengths and areas for development and to direct future learning and teaching to support the student's development of knowledge and skills.

As such, the direct observation is both a point of assessment and a learning activity and should be undertaken collaboratively with the student to reduce anxiety and empower their self-assessment. It can be helpful to break the direct observation into three sections: prior to, during and after the direct observation: the PDA model of direct observation.

Prior to a direct observation

The planning of a direct observation begins in supervision. Collaborative discussion that takes account of the student's feelings and ideas should consider when the direct observations take place. The collaborative discussion should then focus on what will be observed in each direct observation. It is good practice to ensure that the direct observations facilitate the observation of a breadth of social work interventions, for example, a home visit, an interprofessional meeting and an assessment. Referring back to the exchange model of assessment (Smale et al, 1993), it is important to remember that the student is an expert on their caseload and should be able to direct the practice educator to the best examples of practice. Nevertheless, the practice educator's role is to review their suggestions to ensure that neither too much nor too little is being proposed. Finally, the collaborative discussion should consider what is to be assessed within the direct observation. This can be task-centred, to complete a certain activity; skill-centred, to demonstrate an identified learning need; or assessment-criteria centred, where a number of the PCF domains (BASW, 2018) are the focus of the assessment. However, these should be both clear and concise, with a limit of no more than four objectives to be agreed upon.

Student **development exercise**

Prior to your student's first direct observation, ask them to write down three skills that they want feedback on from the direct observation. Ask them why they chose these three skills.

» Is it because they are confident that they will get positive feedback about the skills?

» Is it because they are anxious about the skills and want to know how they are developing?

» Is it because they want you to see that they are struggling and dare not tell you?

Explore with the student their sense of self that they develop from this discussion.

After the planning in supervision, the student will be tasked with preparing for the direct observation. The practical preparation should include liaising with the service user to discuss informed consent to the direct observation and arranging a time and date that is suitable for all parties. The reflective preparation for the student is to reflect on each of the agreed objectives for the direct observation and identify their existing strengths, areas for development and areas that they would specifically like feedback on.

As the student's participation in planning and preparing the direct observation both facilitate the ability to demonstrate knowledge and skills, most particularly professionalism, communication and reflective practice, this first section of the direct observation also creates assessment opportunities.

During a direct observation

It is during the direct observation that the practice educator is able to assess the student against the pre-agreed objectives. The ethical dilemma of note-taking while observing is raised here, as it can be off-putting for the student but can enhance the evidence-based feedback; whether or not to take notes is an individual decision. Furthermore, the location of the practice educator should be considered, and it is often preferable where possible to be out of the direct eyeline of the student.

It is important within the direct observation to allow the student to take the lead from the start of the appointment. They should introduce the observer and reiterate informed consent for the observer's attendance. The role of the practice educator during a direct observation is that of an observer and the student should be able to complete the intervention as though they were not there. Nevertheless, it may become necessary for the practice educator to intervene. This may be on a minimal basis, such as providing a piece of information that the student did not have. Alternatively, it may be on a substantial basis, where the practice educator feels that the student has lost their way and can offer nothing further or that the student is placing the service user at risk of harm. In the former case, this is often in response to a student referring to the practice educator; however, this should be kept to a minimum or summarised at the end of the student's intervention. However, in the latter case, it is up to the practice educator's discretion when to intervene; they should be aware that as it is likely to affect the student's confidence, it should be done tactfully and sensitively.

After a direct observation

Immediately after the direct observation, verbal feedback should be provided, and time for this should be allocated in the planning stage. In a confidential space, the practice educator should first ask the student how they felt it went, which is an initial self-assessment. The practice educator should then provide positive and constructive feedback to the student on the learning outcomes, using the SCORE model outlined in Chapter 3. If the practice educator had to intervene in the direct observation, this should be reflectively discussed during the initial verbal feedback.

It is critical that both practice educator and student complete the written task immediately to ensure that the feedback and assessment are valid and reliable. It should be on the university's required form to ensure that it meets the assessment criteria. Finally, further reflective discussion in supervision soon after the direct observation is useful to both support the student and facilitate further learning from the direct observation.

Professional **development prompt**

>> Using either the example in the case example of a direct observation of Sophia or drawing on your own direct of observation of a student, reflect on how you could facilitate a safe environment for learning and assessment **p**rior to, **d**uring and **a**fter the direct observation.

It is important here that you reflect on good practice and the ethical dilemmas that you may face as a practice educator undertaking a direct observation. While most direct observations will go as planned and result in observation of good practice by the student, it is the preparation for the unexpected that develops your practice education knowledge and skills. Practice educators often ask if it is okay to retrospectively count a co-worked visit or meeting as a direct observation, as it can reduce the student's stress and facilitate the assessment of what may be considered practice that is their norm. However, this does mean that the planning and preparation prior to direct observation are not incorporated, resulting in missed learning and assessment opportunities. As such, it is recommended that there is never more than one impromptu direct observation within the social work student placement and it is only implemented with the full agreement of the student and service user.

Impact **of the pandemic**

Direct observations are traditionally undertaken of in-person appointments with a service user or other professional(s). However, remote intervention has become increasingly common. Where the mode of intervention with a service user is normally through remote communication, the student can be observed through remote communication, albeit still with the service user's informed consent. Indeed, this can make it easier for both student (as they are less obviously being observed) and practice educator (as it reduces the time constraints) and widens the breadth of observational opportunities by adding an additional format that can be observed (Beesley and Taplin, 2023). As before, a range of interventions and meetings should be observed, and at least one should be a face-to-face direct observation.

Assessing the student's social work values

The practice educator is required to assess the student's knowledge and skills in relation to social work values, ethics, oppression, discrimination, human rights and social justice (PCF 2, 3 and 4) (BASW, 2018) both diagnostically and formatively as the placement progresses and summatively at the end of placement. The practice educator can assess the student through both their actions and their words. Firstly, where the student is respectful of the service user and practises in a non-judgemental and anti-discriminatory manner using a person-centred and empowering approach, this can be assessed through service user and colleague feedback and direct and informal observation of practice. In relation to the student's words, while the student's written reflections provide physical evidence, verbal reflective discussions in social work student supervision and the team room will provide more subjective and less tangible evidence where the practice educator may reflect on the student's attitude or perspective. Nevertheless, provisional to remaining evidence based (*'when talking about Mrs E, the student expressed concerns about the smell of the house and dog hairs, which raised concerns about her values in relation to cleanliness'*), these discussion-based assessments remain an important part of the practice educator's assessment of the student's social work values.

However, this prompts the question of what the practice educator should do where they have concerns about the student's value base, as they can be harder to evidence than, for example, a home visit not being recorded on the service user's file. It is important to not confuse the process of exploration of value conflicts (Hollinrake, 2018) by the student, where they may express personal values that conflict with professionals as part of a developmental process, with a student who does not engage in reflective practice in relation to their values. Chapter 7 outlines the process to follow where the practice educator identifies significant areas for development, which the practice educator should refer to if they have concerns about the student's value base. However, in order to assist you in identifying what would constitute a concern about the student's value base, consideration can be given to a number of factors.

Professional **development prompt**

Where you have concerns about the student's value base, assess the student's values against:

» the appropriate assessment level within PCF Domains 2, 3 and 5, the BASW Code of Ethics and the Social Work England Professional Standards;

» the placement agency statement of values;

» your own personal and professional values;

» the service user's rights, and colleague and service user feedback;

» the student's willingness to reflect on their values.

Reflective discussion with your mentor will enable an objective assessment of the student's social work values and facilitate decision making.

Where the practice educator has provided constructive feedback and facilitated the activities within this section on student social work values, and the student is not engaging reflectively with the development of their professional values, then the practice educator should initiate the procedures in Chapter 7.

Academic work

Practice educators often play a pivotal role in helping the student choose appropriate pieces of work to present as evidence, validating the student's practice and ensuring it conforms to agency procedures, including anonymising the portfolio. If the practice educator is working towards assessing the student in a holistic fashion, which involves understanding a student's thinking, it is vital that they both enable them to create good-quality written pieces of reflective work and assess its value in demonstrating their developing knowledge and skills.

Furthermore, some education providers may invite the practice educator to grade a piece of written work. This can be a difficult task for a practice educator with limited to no experience in marking and with no comparative created through marking a number of students at the same time. Here, it is wise to seek support from the university, who will often have an assessment mark grid to guide the marker. When marking an assignment, do refer back to the discussion of cognitive bias; it is likely that the practice educator will be a more generous marker for a student who has engaged well with the placement and learning opportunities, and less generous where there have been areas for development or an acrimonious supervisory relationship. Nevertheless, the practice educator will not be required to mark in isolation, and the academic tutor is likely to be more experienced at both marking and supporting the practice educator to agree the final grade.

Interim and final assessment

The interim, often also known as the mid-point, meeting and report can be the first formal assessment stage in the social work placement. Given the emphasis on progressive and developmental assessment, the interim review process can be seen as a vital tool for the review of the student's progress and planning for the second half of the placement. This is another opportunity for the student to contribute actively to their learning and assessment, and good practice would be for the facilitation of collaborative and reflective discussion on the assessment criteria, usually the PCF (BASW, 2018) domains, shortly before the interim report is due to be written. The interim report should be written prior to the interim meeting, as it triggers a closer reflection on the development of knowledge and skills within each domain and is often the catalyst for increased confidence in the student's capability or identification of gaps. The interim meeting enables a review of the learning objectives identified in the pre-placement (PLA) meeting and discussion of the student's strengths and development of knowledge and skills in the first half of the placement, thus boosting the student's self-confidence. It also facilitates discussion of the areas for development, with provision for the drawing up of new learning objectives and clear plans for how they will be supported.

The culmination of the assessment process for a practice educator is the writing of a final report which reflects the student's development of knowledge and skills throughout the placement and across each of the PCF domains (BASW, 2018). It is essential to ensure that the final assessments are informed by evidence; they may include both a cross-reference to student's evidence cited in the placement portfolio and examples of work undertaken that are not included. By the student providing evidence that demonstrates that they have analysed the thinking behind their work, the practice educator is able to undertake a summative assessment of the student's professional role, knowledge and value base, and ensure that the required skills are in place. Social work students in England are required to pass each PCF domain, and the practice educator should reflect on whether or not the student has met the capability as set out in the appropriate placement level for each domain. The final report is usually required to be given to the student on the last day of the placement and generally consists of the following items.

» A summary of the outcome of the assessment, including if the student has passed or failed the placement.

» Assessment of each domain, where practice educators provide both examples and qualitative description of practice to support their overall assessment.

» The holistic assessment, where practice educators record their overarching judgement of students.

» Identification of strengths and areas for development, including future learning goals.

» An opportunity for the student, tutor and (where appropriate) on-site supervisor to comment on the assessment by the practice educator.

It can be seen that a holistic assessment decision is in no way a purely subjective decision but is in fact an evidence-based summation of assessment throughout the placement. Indeed, the final report should present no surprises, and should embody the flow from the initial PLA meeting through to the interim review. It should also be forward facing to link to the next level of learning or practice.

Collaborative assessment

Collaboration in social work placements has been discussed in previous chapters, and here we return to the notion that the assessment of the student should be undertaken collaboratively, as illustrated in Figure 6.3. Earlier in the chapter the notion of triangulation (Shardlow and Doel, 1993) was introduced, where a collaborative approach to the student's assessment enriched the assessment outcomes. Here we consider the important role that all stakeholders play in the student's assessment.

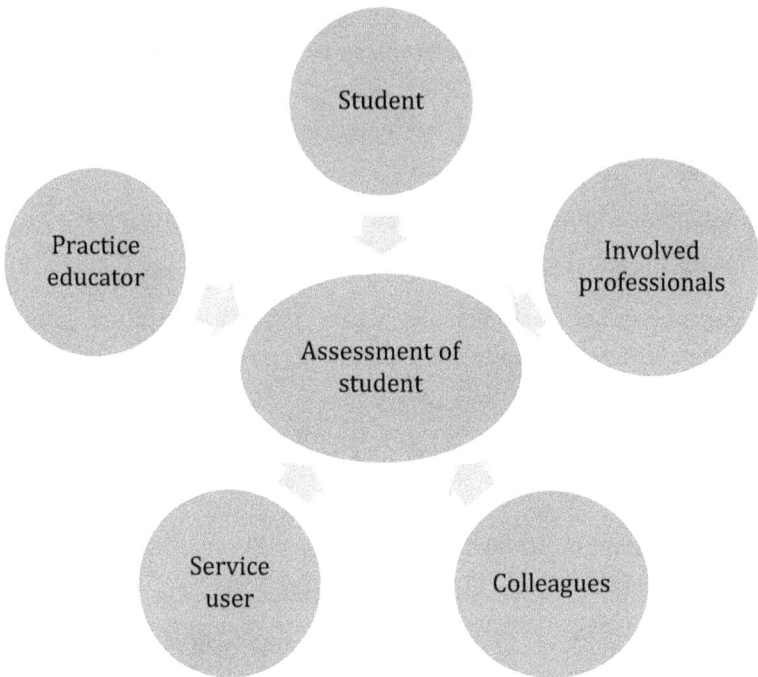

Figure 6.3 Collaborative student assessment

Practice educator

As has been discussed throughout this chapter, the practice educator has responsibility for the final summative assessment of the student at the end of the placement. Furthermore, they have overall responsibility for the diagnostic and formative assessment of the student throughout the placement. However, they should not see assessment as a solo activity and should ensure open communication with the other stakeholders: the student, service users, colleagues and other professionals. Furthermore, as co-ordinator of the assessment process, the practice educator should support the other stakeholders in the assessment process.

Involvement of the student

One of the fundamental tenets of good practice proposed within this book is that the student should be involved in all stages of the placement process, enabling a collaborative approach that engages the principles of andragogical learning (Knowles, 1973). The planning and organisation of the assessment process should be a shared process between practice educator and student (Williams and Rutter, 2021). Indeed, the PCF

Domain 1, professionalism, emphasises the centrality of supervision and states that by the end of the first placement the student *'should recognise and act on own learning needs in response to practice experience'* (BASW, 2018). This participation in the diagnostic assessment is important as it is only by assessing and acknowledging learning needs that a student can begin to address them, as discussed in the section on the conscious competence model (Burch, 1970) in Chapter 3.

This can be undertaken collaboratively in social work student supervision where the practice educator begins reflective discussion on the development of knowledge and skills by asking *'how do you think you are getting on with this?'* Here the student is stimulated to reflect on their self-assessment and to take the lead in the discussion. It is important to remember, of course, that where the student is overly confident or negative in reflecting on their practice, it is the practice educator's role to tactfully but assertively redirect their self-assessment. Nevertheless, the practice educator will often experience increased insight and enhanced diagnostic and formative assessment of the student through the resulting discussion. In addition, many universities require the student to self-assess their development within each of the PCF domains (BASW, 2018) in addition to the provision of evidence, aligning with the concept of capability rather than competence discussed at the start of the chapter.

Involving the student in self-assessment should be a central consideration for practice educators. Williams and Rutter (2021) make the point that the dynamics produced by the assessment element of the practice educator role is where the power imbalance between student and practice educator can most obviously manifest itself. The principle therefore of sharing responsibility and enabling students to develop the tools and confidence to self-assess and contribute to the developmental process is a key to maximising the sharing of power. Indeed, when considering the models of assessment (Smale et al, 1993), although the questioning and procedural models of assessment have a place, the exchange model of assessment appears to be the most productive. The exchange model views the student as the expert in themselves and the practice educator as the expert in social work knowledge and skills. It is the collaborative exchange of both of these elements that reduces the power differential, involves the student and enhances the assessment process.

Involvement of people with lived experience

It is important here to remind the reader that people with lived experience are important stakeholders within social work education (King-Owen, 2020) as they provide a grounded reality (Irvine et al, 2015). Wallcraft et al (2012) conclude that although the involvement of people with lived experience is now common in social work education, their involvement is weakest in the area of assessment. The service user will provide a different perspective on student assessment on placement than other stakeholders, as they may have been the beneficiary of good-quality service provision or may, sadly, be able to reflect of the impact of less desirable service provision by the student. Nevertheless, involvement should be *'meaningful'* (Calvin Thomas, 2014), and thus superficial involvement that is tokenistic should be avoided as it is demeaning to the person. As such, the involvement of the service user in the student's assessment should be a placement-wide activity, and may include involvement in induction, intervention feedback and within each direct observation.

The involvement of the service user should begin at the start of the placement. This could involve inviting the person to provide initial feedback to the student in induction visits as part of a diagnostic assessment because hearing about the impact of self will support the student's development of professionalism and emotional intelligence. As the placement progresses and the student is allocated casework, this should include collection of feedback on a regular basis throughout the intervention, both when asked and when they wish to provide it. Considering that most social work intervention is subject to regular review, then at the point service user progress is reviewed, so too should the student's involvement. It is important to ensure that all allocated service users are provided with the opportunity to provide feedback, rather than the hand-picked ones who would be expected to provide glowing feedback. Indeed, it can be argued that constructive feedback that includes mention of both good practice and suggestions for improvement enhances learning more than a report that suggests that everything was perfect.

Service user involvement in the assessment of the student through a direct observation can include asking the service user if they have assessment objectives upon which they will assess the student's performance prior to the direct observation and reviewing them with the service user after the direct observation (Calvin Thomas, 2014). Such assessment objectives for the service user may include if they felt heard, valued and supported. While it is helpful for the student to be present in the development of the assessment objectives in the discussion with the service user prior to the direct observation, the service user should be afforded the choice of whether or not the student is present during their provision of open and honest constructive feedback in the discussion after the direct observation. If the student is not present, they should be provided with this feedback by the practice educator soon after the direct observation, and the student should be afforded reflective discussion to ensure experiential learning (Kolb, 1984) from the feedback.

Professional **development prompt**

Reflect on how you currently involve service users within the assessment of the student.

» How can you involve the service user more in the student's assessment?

» Think about the benefits and the challenges that you may face and discuss your ideas with a service user.

It is likely that your first reflection will raise some possibly tokenistic activities, for example, that the student asks one service user to complete a brief form that is put into their evidence portfolio and no further action is taken. The professional development prompt is designed to develop your service user involvement beyond the basic minimum and to ensure that it has meaning (Calvin Thomas, 2014). In order to make the service user involvement in assessment meaningful, the practice educator should ensure that it stimulates reflective collaborative discussion within social work student supervision that leads to the development of knowledge and skills. Finally, by having their own discussion with a service user about the ideas, the practice educator is embracing service user involvement in their own practice.

Involvement of colleagues and other involved professionals

As has been discussed earlier in this chapter, cognitive bias should be avoided, and there is no better way to do this than to *'get a second opinion'*. This can be done by asking colleagues and other professionals to provide written or verbal feedback on their experiences of working with the student. Furthermore, this enables the student's assessment to cover interventions when the practice educator is not present, meaning that the power dynamic is not as prevalent. The principles outlined throughout this chapter should be utilised when asking colleagues and other professionals to be involved in the student's assessment, so that the student is clear of who will be undertaking the assessment; when, why and where the assessment will be undertaken; and in what way it will be undertaken, using the TAPE model of assessment (Stone, 2018).

Finally, consideration should be given to where the practice educator is working with an on-site supervisor (OSS). Here it is less likely that the practice educator will be situated in the placement office and they will not have the benefit of informal ongoing assessment. As such, the OSS assessment of the student's capability against each of the PCF domains (BASW, 2018) will be critical. It is recommended that the practice educator and OSS meet on a regular basis to discuss the student's progress, which should be fed back to the student too.

Conclusion

This chapter is designed to support the development of the practice educator's knowledge and skills in relation to the assessment of the student on social work placement. It reviewed key principles that underpin a fair assessment process, assessment criteria, assessment within the social work placement and collaborative assessment.

The chapter concluded by asking the reader to reflect on their assessment skills and to ponder whether by becoming a practice educator they are now a gatekeeper for the future generation of the profession of social work. Their role is to assist social work students to develop knowledge and skills to enable them to become qualified social workers who demonstrate good practice and social work values, as discussed in Chapter 4. Practice educators also need to quality assure that students have indeed met the required Professional Standards (SWE, 2020) to ensure ongoing service provision that meets the needs of the vulnerable service users with whom the profession works.

Taking it further

Stone, C (2018) Transparency of Assessment in Practice Education: The TAPE Model. *Social Work Education*, 37(8): 977–94. The model introduced in this article reflects on the importance of practice educators being explicit in their assessment of students to engage students and enhance assessment outcomes.

Williams, S and Rutter, L (2021) *The Practice Educator's Handbook*. London: Learning Matters. Part 3 of this accessible book focuses on Domain C of the PEPS (BASW, 2022) standards that relates to the assessment of students.

Chapter 7

Dealing with placement challenges

Chapter aims

» To consider the range of challenges that may arise during a social work placement, and the role of the practice educator in managing these situations.

» To explore the processes and procedures to be followed in supporting a student where there are identified areas for development.

» To equip the practice educator with knowledge and skills to assist them in such situations.

Critical **questions**

» How do you address challenges in placement to enable a collaborative learning environment?

» How do you weigh strengths and areas for development where the student is 'marginal'?

Introduction

This chapter meets elements of all the Practice Educator Professional Standards for social work (PEPS) (BASW, 2022) domains and the statement of values, as it requires the practice educator to work with others; teach, facilitate, support and assess student development; and be aware of their own development as a practice educator because addressing placement challenges often requires more nuanced responses. It is important to remember that, although this chapter is written from the perspective of what the practice educator can do to address any challenges within the placement, the student is also required to contribute to the resolution of issues discussed within this chapter.

In the majority of cases, the practice placement will progress smoothly, and the student will be enthusiastic and motivated to learn, demonstrating a developing level of knowledge, skills and values. However, some practice educators will experience challenges within their placement provision. These can be placement based, and the first half of the chapter focuses on common placement challenges and offer advice on how to resolve them. The second half of the chapter focuses on the role of the practice educator in collaboratively working with the student to address the area for development and, ultimately, what to do when the student does not meet the assessment criteria. It includes the areas of procedural processes, supervision, action plan meeting, placement suspension, marginal students and failing students.

Dealing with placement challenges

While placements will usually run smoothly and effectively, the practice educator's role is to identify and resolve any challenges within the placement. There are a number of difficulties that may arise on placement, and an awareness of potential problems may support the practice educator to avoid them or be able to address them if they arise. It would be naive not to include the impact of the Covid-19 pandemic as a challenge to placement provision. Placement challenges can include:

» difficulty in obtaining a particular type of learning opportunity to meet an assessment criterion or learning need within the placement;

» a significant period of workplace absence of the student or practice educator;

» a period of agency crisis in terms of incoming work or organisational or staff changes within the workplace;

» a delay in obtaining student access to the agency's computer systems;

» the practice educator and student are working at home/in the office at opposite ends of the week;

» the health or personal circumstances of the practice educator or student;

» a difficult supervisory relationship;

» the student feeling that the placement does not meet their placement expectations;

» the attitude or motivation of the student;

» the student not being prepared for the placement;

» poor practice performance of the student;

» poor engagement by the practice educator.

This is not an exhaustive list, and often unexpected challenges arise and surprise us.

Professional **development prompt**

From the above list of potential difficulties that might arise on placement, reflect on:

» which are the most serious potential problems;

» what specific knowledge you might need to help you to deal effectively with each situation;

» what potential action (if any) you might have to take in relation to each issue.

While you may be able to list the severity of the issues above, it will be a subjective ordering. However, it gives you a good idea of what you consider important and hopefully prompts some proactive and reflective preparation to minimise these potential challenges. The challenges can be broadly divided into four areas: the placement setting, the practice educator, the student, and the practice educator–student relationship, each of which will now be discussed. It is important to note here that this is not about allocating blame, but rather about facilitating awareness of how challenges can arise and how they can be addressed.

Placement setting

The first area for consideration that can create challenges to learning opportunities for the student is the placement setting itself. Often there is a sense that these are out of the control of the practice educator, but as discussed in Chapter 2, careful preparation and discussion with colleagues can mitigate some of the issues. A common challenge for practice educators is where the team are experiencing a period of crisis. This can be due to staff shortages created by illness or turnover, and often place more pressure and workload on the practice educator as the team pulls together to ensure work is covered. In this instance, it is helpful for the practice educator to speak to their manager to ensure that their role as practice educator is taken into account when work is redistributed. Furthermore, it is helpful to ringfence supervision time from the start of the placement so that irrespective of the rest of the week the student will have undisturbed time with the practice educator each week. The importance of a daily check-in each morning will be amplified in such a situation and should be prioritised. This is not to say that the practice educator should spread themselves so thin that they go off sick, but rather that when prioritising workload, the student should be considered a high priority. Where the practice educator is unable to fulfil all their prioritised roles, then they should discuss with their mentor if the role of practice educator is realistic at this time. Finally, discussing with the team if anyone can offer support for the student, which should be seen as important for enhancing the student's learning experience in any circumstances, can ensure that they receive support little and often from the team to ensure that they feel valued and supported.

By contrast, while the practice educator may crave a quiet referral period, the student's opportunity to engage with learning activities can be severely restricted where there is no new or appropriate work available for the student to undertake. In this circumstance, the practice educator is required to think creatively and consider co-working so that the student can take the lead in a supported environment in more complex work, or to take on less complex roles within a complex case. Furthermore, discussion with other teams or agencies may create work that the student could become involved in, for example, groupwork in a children's centre or duty work in the assessment team. In addition, the student can be asked to undertake a project, as outlined in the student development exercise below, to enhance learning in other areas, including Professional Capabilities Framework (PCF) Domain 9, professional leadership (BASW, 2018), which can sometimes be difficult to meet in a statutory team.

Student **development exercise**

Ask the student to undertake a project that addresses identified placement need and enables them to develop their knowledge on a topic and then share it with others. This could be:

» visiting another service to deliver information about the placement agency referral criteria service;

» attending a training session and feeding it back to the team in a briefing;

» researching a theory and delivering it to a team meeting;

» researching a service provision and creating a leaflet that could be distributed to service users.

Ask the student to reflect on their learning from the activity.

Where there is organisational change, for example, teams being reconfigured, practice educators often prefer not to have a student. However, it is good to remember that students will experience change throughout their social work careers and learning to deal with it is a skill development in itself. If there is change during the placement period, the practice educator's role is to ensure that the student is fully informed and understands what is happening so that they feel safe, as knowledge is power. There may be some team or individual animosity to the proposed changes that impact the team dynamic or spirit. In this situation, the practice educator should both ask the team to be positive for the sake of the student's learning and discuss it with the student so that they are aware of where any disgruntlement is coming from.

When considering practical issues such as waiting for access to the agency's computer systems or for a previous student to complete their placement to free a desk space, it is important to remember that this may make the student feel unvalued and not part of the team. It is important for the practice educator to advocate regularly (daily if need be) for the resolution of practical issues that will enable the student to engage with learning opportunities. However, in the short term the practice educator can ensure that there are solutions so that the student is not penalised.

Impact of the pandemic

Post-pandemic, many placement providers are operating blended working practices that incorporate both working at home and within the office, often with restricted office space available. Here it will be important for the practice educator, where required, to book two desks so that they can be in the office on the same day as the student, and to co-ordinate diaries to ensure that this happens as often as possible. Where necessary, the option of the student becoming fully office based can be considered. If the student can be in the office and at least one member of the team is with them each day, they would be afforded a natural opportunity to observe good practice and ask questions that would help them to develop their knowledge and skills.

Practice educator

It is imperative that the practice educator is available to the student, but there may be a number of reasons why this is not possible. These might be known factors that can be addressed and planned for in the placement learning agreement meeting, for example, annual leave, compressed hours, a part-time role or health restrictions. In the instance of regular or planned limited availability, it can be helpful to ask within the team for a named person that the student can approach in the practice educator's absence. Where the practice educator is known to be leaving part way through the placement, for example, on maternity leave or for a new job, a clear agreement should be made about who is taking over the role of practice educator and when. It is helpful to schedule a further placement meeting with the student, tutor, old and new practice educator, and mentor and on-site supervisor where appropriate to discuss the handover.

However, there may also be unexpected changes to the practice educator's availability, for example, sick leave or change of role or team. Where it is short-term sickness, the student should be assigned a named person to be able to approach. However, if the sick leave extends beyond a week, the line manager or placement co-ordinator should allocate a temporary practice educator to ensure that the student is not left unsupported, as this can result in drift including the direct observations not being undertaken. Where the practice educator changes role, be that internal promotion, change of team or leaving the placement agency, the practice educator should reflect on whether they are able to continue in their role as practice educator to the student, which is often dependent on the nature of the change of role and the length of placement remaining. In both circumstances, the tutor should be informed and a placement meeting facilitated to ensure clarity of roles where a new practice educator becomes involved.

There can be additional complexity involved in managing placements where an off-site practice educator (OSPE) and on-site supervisor (OSS) model is used. While the involvement of two supervisors can enable the student to benefit from a richer range of skills, knowledge and experience, the OSPE needs to ensure that there is clarity of respective roles, tasks and responsibilities in order to ensure the placement functions effectively. The need for regular three-way meetings is therefore essential to ensure any issue or concerns are discussed promptly and openly and that the student's development of knowledge and skill is being reviewed. It is important to remember here that while the OSPE has the lead in the assessment, it should be a collaborative assessment, as discussed in Chapter 6.

Finally, consideration has to be given to whether or not the practice educator has the knowledge and skills to practice educate the student. Research has identified that students develop their knowledge and skills best where the practice educator is versatile and flexible (Litvack et al, 2010; Brodie and Williams, 2013; Beesley, 2022); supportive (Lefevre, 2005; Kanno and Koeske, 2010; Litvack et al, 2010; Brodie and Williams, 2013; Miehls et al, 2013; Beesley, 2022); approachable (Litvack et al, 2010; Brodie and Williams, 2010); reliable, open and honest

(Brodie and Williams, 2013); and passionate and motivated (Ketner et al, 2017). Research has also illustrated that a nuanced student-centred and non-judgemental approach, where the practice educator is responsive to students' individual needs, is considered the most appropriate way in which to develop the student's knowledge and skills (Beesley, 2022). Where the practice educator feels that they do not have these skills, discussion with the mentor would be appropriate to ensure that they are providing the student with the best approach to practice educating. The practice educator's ability to facilitate learning, manage the placement, promote reflection, and to teach and link theory to practice are all key aspects that affect the quality of placement learning from the perspective of social work students (Lefevre, 2005).

Professional **development exercise**

Reflect on your practice educator style in relation to the characteristics in the paragraph above. It can be helpful to ask your student and your mentor for their assessment of these characteristics too.

» What do you think your strengths are?

» What do you think your areas for development are? Talk to your mentor and discuss how you can develop these characteristics.

By having an emotionally intelligent awareness of your strengths and areas for development in relation to practice education knowledge and skills, you will be able to enhance your practice and avoid potential challenges.

Student

As discussed in Chapter 3, social work students on placement are considered to be adult learners and therefore to be impacted by Knowles' (1973) andragogical principles, meaning that they are orientated to learning. A significant challenge within the placement, then, is when the student is not engaging with the learning activities available within the placement. This can be caused by a number of reasons which the practice educator will need to explore, understand and address to support the student's ability to engage. Firstly, this can come about when the student does not feel prepared for the placement. This can be due to inadequate pre-placement teaching or a lack of engagement by the student with the pre-placement teaching. In this instance, the practice educator should explore what the student does and does not know so that the appropriate level of support can be provided, thus ensuring that it is student-centred and meets their individual needs (Beesley, 2022). Furthermore, it can be helpful to support them to revisit pre-placement teaching materials or direct them to one of the available books on preparation for and engagement with the placement. However, it may be that the lack of preparation is because the student has not addressed practical matters and is distracted; for example, they may not have organised adequate childcare, are still working full time on top of the placement hours, or they have outstanding academic work. Here the practice educator should discuss with the student how these matters can be addressed and could even consider a short suspension of the placement to enable resolution if short-term flexibility is insufficient.

However, a challenge can be where the student expresses that the placement does not meet their expectations, including requested placement service provision area or location. It is important for the practice educator to know that students' placements can be anywhere within the agreed geographical area, which can be quite significant, and that no matching beyond requesting an adults' or children's placement can be guaranteed. As such, if the student is matched with a placement that is both a lengthy commute and not in their preferred service user provision, they may feel disgruntled to be matched with the placement. Furthermore, it should be noted that Social Work England (2019) placement requirements stipulate that students should undertake two contrasting placements, which is normally translated as one adults' and one children's placement. This may mean that the student is wishing to become an adults' social worker, but has a first placement within children's, so is less engaged. This does not excuse lack of engagement with learning opportunities but may help the practice educator to understand it. In this situation, time should be spent in supervision reflecting on transferability of skills and the generic nature of social work education. Furthermore, the practice educator can explore what service provision area the student is interested in and, where possible, direct student case allocation in that direction as service provision is often multi-faceted. For example, where a student wanted to work in a mental health service but is allocated a domestic abuse placement, the student could be allocated work where a parent or child is also accessing mental health services, which would develop the student's understanding of services that work with mental health services.

Student **development exercise**

In supervision, ask the student what they had initially expected from the placement in terms of:

» the level and type of work to be undertaken;

» how they would get on with the placement team;

» how they would learn knowledge and skills.

Repeat this and ask what their experiences have been in each area.

This should be used as the basis for a reflective discussion where you are able to identify differences in expectations and explore both the basis for the assumptions and the reality of learning on placement to facilitate mutual understanding.

A further cause of lack of engagement with learning activities can be where the student feels overwhelmed by the placement or overly confident within their own knowledge and skills. Where the student feels overwhelmed, it can be helpful for the practice educator to break down the tasks into smaller activities, using the SMART principles (Doran, 1981), and engaging an enhanced educational function in supervision to ensure that the student feels empowered by understanding what is required of them. Where the student feels overly confident, revisiting the nature of the PCF (BASW, 2018) as a developmental tool and reiterating the need to see development in each domain irrespective of initial ability can be helpful, as can asking the student to reflect empathically on how their self might be perceived by others.

Finally, reflecting back to the learning styles (Honey and Mumford, 1992) outlined in Chapter 3, collaborative reflective discussion should be undertaken in social work student supervision to determine if the student is not engaging with the learning activities because they do not meet their learning style. For instance, where the student is a theoretical or reflective learner and they have been asked to just get on with it, they may feel unable to do this without having time to prepare and understand what is required of them. Similarly, consideration should be given to the student's individual learning needs, for example, referring back to the discussion in Chapter 3 on the impact of disability or cultural educational history and adjusting the practice education provision to ensure that it meets their learning needs.

It is important to note that, with practice educator input, the student is likely to reflect on their own attitude and begin to engage with the learning activities. However, if the student's attitude persists to be one that does not engage with the learning activities, for any reason, after feedback and support is offered by the practice educator, then the practice educator should raise concerns about the student's ability to meet PCF Domain 1, professionalism (BASW, 2018), and the process below should be activated.

The practice educator–student relationship

As discussed in Chapter 5 on supervision, the supervisory relationship has been found to be critical to the successful development of knowledge and skills within placement and supervision (Roulston et al, 2018; Ketner et al, 2017; Yeung et al, 2021; Beesley, 2022). Therefore, when considering challenges that may arise in the social work placement, the supervisory relationship must be discussed. Where students fail their placement, they often cite the relationship with the practice educator as a significant contributing factor. Indeed, a weak supervisory relationship can prevent the student from accessing collaborative reflective learning or asking for help, thus limiting their ability to develop their knowledge and skills (Litvack et al, 2010; Beesley, 2022).

We cannot get on with everybody, but as social workers we are skilled at engaging a wide range of service users. The term *'personality clash'* should be recognised as an unhelpful concept that is best avoided as it diverts discussion away from a more objective analysis and direct naming of the issues of concern. While the student must also engage with the relationship, the practice educator is the lead within the relationship, as they hold the authority. The role of practice educator comes with inherent power as the assessor of the student's placement outcome. As has been discussed throughout the book, this can be reduced through collaborative practice education and open and honest discussion. The practice learning agreement meeting offers an opportunity for the initial introduction of information about what procedures and sources of support are available to the student (and the practice educator) if disagreements or difficulties arise during the placement. This can be supplemented by further discussion in induction and when drawing up a supervision agreement with the student and revisited throughout the placement. Nevertheless, it has been identified that the supervisory relationship is impactful (Roulston et al, 2018; Ketner et al, 2017; Yeung et al, 2021; Beesley, 2022) on the ability to explore areas for development openly and honestly. It is important that the student is empowered so that they are able to engage in honest communication with the practice educator from an early stage of the placement, which will enable them to remain engaged if significant areas for development become apparent.

Professional **development prompt**

- » What do you think might be barriers to the student engaging with you as the practice educator?

- » How will you redress the power imbalance between yourself and the student?

This develops further the professional development prompt above that asked you to reflect on your knowledge and skills as a practice educator and consider the holistic issues that might affect the supervisory relationship. This furthers the emotionally intelligent self-awareness that enables you to provide a higher quality of support to the student.

Suspension of placement

The student may request a brief placement break, perhaps due to illness. However, the practice educator, as facilitator of the learning environment, has the option to suspend the placement if they feel it is merited. This can be because they do not feel that the student is *'fit to practise'* because of their health or may be because there has been an incident(s) that requires investigation before the placement can proceed.

In the first instance, it may be that the student lacks the emotional intelligence to reflect on their self and ability to engage in the short term with the placement; for example, when they experience a bereavement. Indeed, professionalism can be assessed as impacted where the student has *'health conditions that have not been managed effectively and may put people at risk'* (SWE, 2021).

This is not to say that a short break would not result in the student returning to the placement and completing it successfully. However, the practice educator may have to be assertive with the student that the service user needs to be safeguarded, and indeed the student's health and well-being too. This decision should be taken collaboratively in discussion with the student and university tutor, and mentor and OSS where appropriate. An agreed date for return should be set and flexibly reviewed. Finally, a return to placement meeting should be held that provides support and clarity for the student, which may include a phased return if appropriate and coping strategies to prevent the need for any further placement suspensions.

However, a placement suspension can also be implemented if there is an incident or series of incidents or behaviours that raises concerns about the student's *'fitness to practise'* (SWE, 2021). This would only be if the student's practice is regarded as unsafe, unethical, dangerous or damaging to the degree that it places service users at risk; is in contradiction to the placement agency's employee procedures such that if the student were an employee, they would be suspended from work; raises concerns within the social work educator policies and procedures; or meets the Social Work England (2021) fitness to practise criteria for investigation. An example of this might be where a student has accessed service user records without permission where they are not involved or had a personal involvement.

This decision would need to be taken with the tutor and the practice educator's mentor, line manager and/or placement co-ordinator. It is highly likely that the student will be anxious that their placement will be terminated, and the practice educator should keep them informed throughout the decision-making process and subsequent investigation of their practice. It may be helpful for the student to access independent support at the time and they can be directed to the National Union of Students (NUS) for support and guidance. The placement agency and/or university will next undertake an investigation into the practice concerns raised to ensure that an informed decision can be made, which will include speaking to the student to ensure that they are heard. Finally, an action plan meeting will be scheduled, where clear agreement will be developed collaboratively with the student as to how they can address the areas for development and the support that they will receive. This would occur before the placement resumed and a return to placement date agreed. The action plan would be reviewed as per the discussion below. However, if the issue cannot be satisfactorily resolved the decision may be taken at the additional placement meeting to terminate the placement.

Supporting a student where there are identified areas for development

For most practice educators, the summative assessment of the student will result in a pass recommendation at the end of the placement. However, during any individual student's period of practice learning, the practice educator is likely to be required to identify areas for development and to support the student to address them. Indeed, one could argue that if the student has no identified areas for development during the length of the placement then either the placement is not sufficiently challenging for the student, or the practice educator and student are not engaging in reflective, collaborative experiential learning. A range of difficulties can arise over the course of a placement, from a fairly minor issue that can be promptly resolved, to a major issue of concern such as an incident of serious professional misconduct by a student that may result in the immediate suspension and perhaps subsequent termination of the student's placement. Early recognition and an open, shared discussion of the problem, followed by prompt implementation of a strategy to deal with the problem, are often key.

Impact **of the pandemic**

The impact of blended placements can be that the student is able to mask their areas for development and the practice educator will need to remain vigilant to where the student is avoiding informal reflective discussion, supervision or assessment. Where this is the case, setting clear timescales and expectations will aid both the practice educator and the student.

Most practice educators express anxiety around having to deal with difficulties relating to a student's poor practice or having to assess a student as having failed their placement. However, adopting a strategy of delay in dealing with an issue of concern in the hope that any problem will eventually resolve itself is rarely a successful one. This section develops the practice educator's understanding of supporting a student where there are identified areas for development, and covers the areas of procedural processes, supervision, action plan meeting, marginal students and failing students.

Procedural processes

Social work students on placement are subject to a range of policies and procedures, including those of the university, the placement provider and Social Work England. Firstly, each university has a placement-level specific practice learning, or placement, handbook, often in the form of a weblink, which the practice educator will be directed to at the start of the placement. The placement handbook contains information about the relevant assessment requirements, learning outcomes and procedures for the placement. These are helpful for the practice educator to refer to in order to ensure that they are fulfilling the course and placement learning expectations within the placement. When there are areas for development, the placement handbook will provide guidance on meeting and recording expectations, and the tutor can offer further guidance if required. However, these are supplemented by university policies and procedures, such as attendance and fitness to practice procedure, which can be accessed via the relevant website. Most often when these are triggered, the practice educator would be advised by the tutor of any expectation on them.

Furthermore, the placement policies and procedures would apply to the student and their practice. This would guide the practice educator in practice expectations, but the university process would replace any placement disciplinary processes. Finally, while social work students do not register with Social Work England, they are expected to practice in accordance with the Professional Standards (SWE, 2020). Any issues to do with professional suitability regarding social work students would be referred to Social Work England after discussion with all involved parties. The practice educator's flowchart in Figure 7.1 provides an overview of the processes that are generally followed when areas for development are identified within the placement.

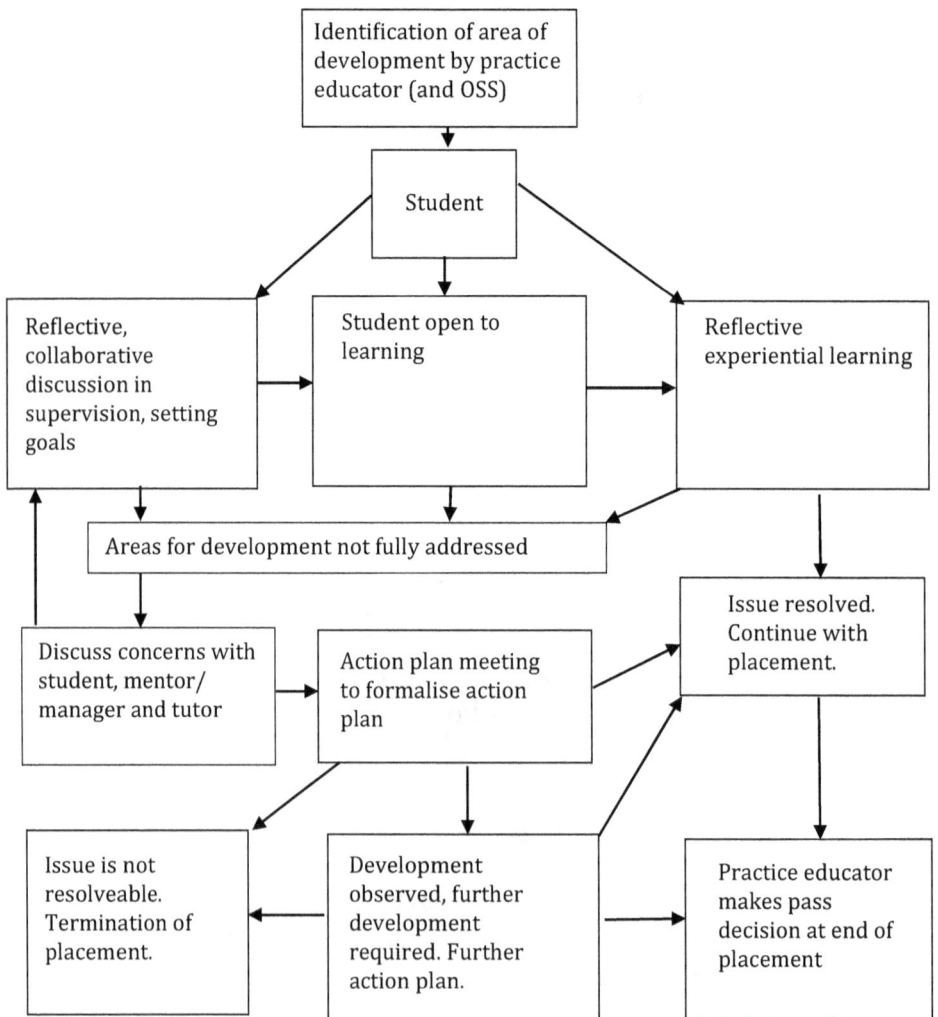

Figure 7.1 Practice educator's flowchart

It may be useful to view social work students as existing on a continuum (ranging from excellent–good–satisfactory–marginal–borderline–failing) as this acknowledges that at any point during the placement, a student can potentially move in either direction along the continuum. This means being open to the possibility that the student can markedly improve or progress from a marginal or potentially failing situation to making satisfactory progress if given the right support. Equally, the student may alternatively continue to move in the direction of an increasing level of concern regarding their progress despite a range of measures being put in place to support the student in their learning, and the practice educator may therefore need to make a fail recommendation.

The use of a case example will be used to illustrate the journey from identification of areas for development as this section develops.

Addressing areas for development in supervision

When the practice educator undertakes a formative assessment and finds that there are areas for development for the student, it is important that they share this assessment quickly and clearly. The first point of discussion should be between the practice educator and the student, for local resolution within supervision. The shared discussion and naming of the concern should be recorded in supervision minutes, an initial plan of action agreed, and a timescale for reviewing progress agreed. At this stage, returning to Chapter 3 on enabling learning is helpful for the practice educator, as their role is to provide robust and constructive feedback, support the student to identify and be ready to engage with the areas for development, and to empower the student to address the areas for development.

Case **example**

Karen is a social work student undertaking her first placement in an independent sector agency. Within a few weeks of the start of the placement, the practice educator identified that Karen appeared to have low motivation for the written aspects of the placement: she was not completing written reflections or case recording within the suggested timescales. When the practice educator raised this, Karen responded that she felt that there was no need for her to write the case notes as a colleague did them before she got to them and that she had just forgotten to email the reflections.

» How would you address this in supervision with Karen?

It is likely that you considered facilitating an open and honest reflective discussion with Karen so that you could understand each other's perspective and expectations. This is an excellent start, as it may have been that Karen viewed learning on placement as '*doing*' and needed support to expand her knowledge. It may be that the practice educator needs to create some additional work and leave the supervision with the task of talking to colleagues about available work.

If the student does not respond to discussion in supervision and practice educator support, then the practice educator should contact their tutor and discuss the student's progress with their mentor and/or manager. This will enable the mentor to offer support and ideas to the practice educator, but also allows reflective discussion that enables the practice educator to ensure that they remain objective. This may result in further work with the student through supervision or in requesting an action plan meeting.

Case **example (continued)**

At the next supervision, the practice educator provides feedback that despite additional learning experiences being offered, she has had feedback from colleagues and observed herself that Karen is not engaging with the learning opportunities.

» Would you raise this differently the following week?

In many ways, social workers are eternal optimists and are trained to give everyone the opportunity to change. The first time you spoke to Karen, she may not have understood the learning opportunity in the placement, but you spoke in supervision last week and clarified this with her. Within this supervision, you may wish to explore if there are any other reasons behind her lack of engagement and offer support to resolve those issues. However, you may also wish to be clear with her that she is expected to engage with learning opportunities and that the formative assessment is that she appears unmotivated. Furthermore, you might set her some mini-objectives to meet, for example, shadow three different workers this week and compare their styles. At this stage, an initial plan of action, which is often considered less formal than an action plan but is an important part of the process, could be agreed upon and noted in the supervision minutes.

In most cases with students, this stage is sufficient to address the areas for development, and no further action is required. Social work students are andragogical learners (Knowles, 1973) and are orientated to learning, so will often be open to hearing the feedback and actioning the areas for development. Of particular note here is that demonstrating how a student engaged with and addressed areas for development with the practice educator is an excellent way to demonstrate PCF Domain 1, professionalism (BASW, 2018), as it shows resilience, determination and ability to take on feedback. At this stage, there is often no need to inform the tutor, but the practice educator may wish to seek support from the practice educator mentor to reassure and inform. Finally, it is recommended that a chronology is created so that the practice educator can track and review how the student engages with addressing the areas for development.

Action plan meeting

If insufficient progress is made in addressing the areas for development effectively, then it may be necessary to hold an additional placement meeting, often called an action plan meeting. It should be noted that the mere mention of an action plan meeting is likely to strike fear into the student, as all they will initially think is that there are 'concerns' and 'I am going to fail the placement'. The role of the practice educator here is to support the student to understand that this should be the start of addressing the areas for development rather than the start of them failing the placement.

Case **example (continued)**

Karen is now a month further into the placement. Karen shadowed colleagues and verbally reflected on their practice, and the practice educator had thought that progress had been made. However, since then Karen has not completed tasks agreed in supervision on a number of her allocated cases and has not been providing her required weekly written reflections. The practice educator has raised this in supervision and set clear actions that have not been met. She now feels that an action plan meeting is required as if Karen does not engage with the learning requirements, there will be insufficient time for her to evidence her capability against each of the PCF domains by the end of the placement.

» How do you share this decision with the student?

The action plan meeting should be chaired by the student's university tutor, and attended by the student, tutor, practice educator and, if appropriate, practice educator mentor and/or OSS. The action plan meeting should discuss any areas for development and create an agreed action plan, outlining the main areas for development and how each issue will be addressed; timescales for implementation and review of each aspect of the plan; and the criteria that will be used to indicate that the required out-come has been successfully achieved. Of note is that the action plan is not the student's sole responsibility to resolve. Instead, the action plan should include what the student needs to do, and what the practice educator, tutor and, if involved, mentor and OSS will do to support the student to develop, as shown in Table 7.1.

Case **example (continued)**

Within Karen's action plan meeting, there is clear discussion about her strengths and areas for development, which focus on engagement with learning activities and reflection on her own practice. Table 7.1 provides an example of how Karen is required to engage with reflection of self, and the support that she will be offered to enable her to achieve this.

Table 7.1 Action plan example

Area for development	Action to be taken	By whom	By when
Critical reflection on own practice	Karen to provide weekly written reflections	Karen	Each Friday
	Practice educator to provide feedback on written reflections	Practice educator	By the following Tuesday
	Discussion in supervision to focus on impact of self on service users	Karen and practice educator	Each weekly supervision
	Provide reading recommendations on organisational skills	Tutor	10 April
	Access university online reflections tutorial (on Virtual Learning Environment [VLE])	Karen	30 April
	Reflection exercises to be explored	Practice educator and practice educator mentor	30 April

In Table 7.1, we can see that the task is broken down into SMART goals, as discussed in Chapter 3. Karen is to provide weekly reflections and is given clear guidance on when this should occur. However, she is also able to see the benefit to completing the tasks: she will receive feedback, which will develop her reflective writing skills further. Finally, all parties will explore creative ways to engage Karen with reflecting skills, as different teaching styles may engage her in different ways.

In the action plan meeting, it is important to reflect on whether there are any barriers to the student's learning. Indeed, in situations where there are identified areas for development, it is especially important to revisit and explore with the student whether there are any as yet unrecognised or unacknowledged barriers that may be impacting on student progress.

The action plan meeting should be minuted, often on an action plan meeting proforma from the university, and given to all parties, including those who did not attend. Finally, a date should be set for a follow-up meeting to review the plan (usually held within four to six weeks). The review period should be long enough to enable the student to evidence development but not too long that they become anxious. Indeed, they should receive feedback from the practice educator between action plan meetings to support the development of their confidence.

At the review action plan meeting, the action plan should be reviewed and each area for development considered. If the area(s) for development have been resolved and the student is 'back on track', there will be no need for any further additional meetings to be held and the rest of the placement can then continue in the usual manner. The action plan should be updated to reflect this decision. However, if the areas for development have not been addressed, or if there are further areas for development that have been identified, the action plan should be updated and a further review meeting booked. Finally, if the action plan meeting determines that the areas for development are unresolvable in the remaining placement period, the placement may need to be terminated and a 'fail' recommendation made.

The practice educator's role within the action planning process is to be knowledge-able: ensure that they are able to provide evidence-based constructive feedback to facilitate the meeting; supportive: by being aware of and responsive to how the student is feeling; and prepared: by providing SMART solutions to support their development. Finally, it should be noted that placements can be extended by a maximum of 20 further days where the practice educator believes that this additional time would enable the student to meet all of the PCF domains (BASW, 2018) and prevent a fail recommendation, but only through agreement with the university which can be discussed in the action plan meeting.

Marginal students

In most cases, the practice educator will be able to make a clear, evidence-based decision where a student is or is not meeting the assessment criteria. However, there are a group of students where it is less clear if a pass or fail recommendation will be made, and the PEPS guidance (2022) refers to these students as *marginal* students. A marginal student can be defined as a student who '*is at risk of failing to reach the standard required*' for the level of the placement (Brandon and Davies, 1979, p 295). At this stage, the weighing up of strengths and areas for development against each PCF domain (BASW, 2018) can be very helpful.

Professional **development prompt**

» Where you are working with a student who you consider marginal, identify strengths and areas for development for each PCF domain.

» Considering the evidence available to you from the student's practice, identify evidence that supports a pass and a fail recommendation for each PCF domain.

» Ensure that you refer back to the appropriate assessment criteria in the Professional Capabilities Framework (BASW, 2018).

» Weigh up your lists and consider which is predominant within each PCF domain: strengths and evidence that supports a pass recommendation or areas for development and evidence that supports a fail recommendation.

This exercise can take a little time and a lot of reflection but is one that can support the practice educator where they have supported the student through the process outlined above and still feel that the student is marginal. It aids the practice educator to recall the placement holistically and solidifies the placement outcome. It can usefully be carried out with a mentor where the practice educator is new to the process, and demonstrates PEPS Domain D3 (BASW, 2022). In addition, the quality assurance requirements of the placement agency will influence what practice is good enough, so the return to the appropriate assessment level is critical.

Furness and Gilligan (2004) found that the impact of the student on service users, professional boundaries and poor use of supervision contributed to students failing their placement, but that these were open to different levels of interpretation. The practice educator will have subjective views on what is good enough practice. In reflecting on the decision making in relation to a marginal student, experienced practice educators often ask themselves some of the following questions to ensure that they are making a fair assessment and are not influenced by cognitive bias (as discussed in Chapter 6). Consider:

» are you clear about what you would regard as a good-enough baseline of practice?

» how would you feel if the student became your mum's social worker or a colleague in your team?

» how would you feel if the student's future practice educator or mentor asked you why you passed or failed this student? Can you justify the decision you make?

» if a student has shown some degree of improvement, are you persuaded that this is good enough because they have tried?

» are you making allowances in terms of lowering your assessment standard regarding what is good enough practice because you are aware that some aspects of the student's learning environment or opportunities were not entirely adequate?

» are you making allowances in terms of the student's personal circumstances?

» are you judging the student too harshly because of their identity?

» is the quality of your relationship with the student impacting your decision making?

» are the possible negative consequences for the student in terms of your assessment decision (such as the cost of repeating a placement and delaying qualification or failing the course) affecting your judgement?

» are you considering that the area for development can be left to the next placement or Assessed and Supported Year in Employment (ASYE) role?

By reflecting on these questions, either individually or with a mentor, the practice educator is able to ensure that the decision made is neither failing to fail the student nor unfairly failing the student. Indeed, it may further support the decision making with a marginal student and either provide reassurance that a pass recommendation is appropriate or confirm that a fail recommendation is correct.

A '*fail*' recommendation

Where the practice educator does not feel that the student has met one or met all of the assessment criteria outlined in the PCF level descriptor (BASW, 2018), then a '*fail*' recommendation should be made. Practice educators tend to come to a fail recommendation in two ways: part way through the placement when it is assessed that the student will not address the areas for development in the remaining placement days available or at the end of the placement when the student has not met the assessment criteria. In either circumstance, it is critical for a fair assessment that the student has been made aware of the areas for development and that the process outlined above has been followed. It is important that the practice educator feels confident and safe to make a fail recommendation where it is merited; seeking support through reflective discussion with the mentor, and OSS where involved, is recommended.

The practice educator makes a final recommendation of the placement outcome both verbally to the student at the end of the placement and in the final report, which is often due on the last day of the placement. In many cases, the student will pass a number of the PCF domains (BASW, 2018), and it is considered important that the student is reminded of what they can do as much as the reasons for the fail recommendation. It is helpful if a chronology is added to the final report that demonstrates when areas for development were assessed and addressed with the student, so that a clear picture of the placement is provided. Finally, it is important that the practice educator makes clear recommendations for work that the student can undertake before a repeat placement opportunity is offered. This will assist the student and the university to ensure that the student uses the time between placements to develop their knowledge, skills and values to enhance their ability to successfully engage with a future placement.

While it should be recognised that the introduction of the PEPS framework in 2013 has significantly enhanced the quality of practice education in England, it is worth reflecting on the complexity of failing a student (Roulston et al, 2022). Finch and Taylor (2013) cite the concept of '*role strain*' as being a factor in why practice educators may find it difficult to fail students. The stress of undertaking and balancing the multiple functions of educator, supporter, case manager and assessor (Doel, 2010) when there are placement challenges can be a considerable source of stress and conflict for practice educators. Finch (2017) recommends the use of courageous conversations to provide both formative and summative assessment feedback, in order to ensure that the student is clear in their understanding of the areas for development and to avoid the practice educator feeling they are unable to fail the student.

Conclusion

This chapter has reflected on supporting a student where there are challenges within the placement that impact on the student's learning opportunities and on supporting a student where there are identified areas for development that need to be addressed. The first half of the chapter focused on challenges that can arise in the placement, and provided both proactive, preventative solutions to minimise impact on the placement and the student, and responsive solutions to resolve a problem if it occurs. It asked the practice educator to reflect on their practice educator skills and develop an awareness of impact of self on the student's ability to engage with learning opportunities and develop knowledge and skills.

In the second half of the chapter, a case example was used to illustrate the journey with a student where there were areas for development. The practice educator role across the different procedural points is to provide constructive feedback and support the student's development of knowledge and skills, as it should not be assumed that it is the student's task to develop these alone. Indeed, a collaborative approach should be undertaken to engage and motivate the student.

Taking it further

Doel, M and Shardlow, S (2018) *The New Social Work Practice: Exercises and Activities for Training and Developing Social Workers*. Abingdon: Routledge. This book provides the reader with a variety of exercises that can be undertaken with the student to stimulate development of knowledge and skills, so is particularly useful for the practice educator who has exhausted their repertoire and is looking for new learning activities to address areas for development.

Finch, J (2017) *Supporting Struggling Students on Placement*. Bristol: Policy Press. This is an excellent and comprehensive guide for supporting students where there are identified areas for development.

Morris, B, Todd, S and Kalmanovitch, A (2022) When the Going Gets Tough: Case Studies of Challenge and Innovation in Canadian Field Education. In Baikady, R, Sajid, S, Nadesan, V and Rezaul Islam, M (eds) *The Routledge Handbook of Field Work Education in Social Work* (pp 156–71).

New Delhi: Routledge. This chapter provides case studies that explore the impact of student mental health, placement insecurity and student financial strain on student engagement and practice educator responses.

Roulston, A, Cleak, H, Nelson, R and Hayes, D (2022) How Power Dynamics and Relationships Interact with Assessment of Competence: Exploring the Experiences of Student Social Workers Who Failed a Practice Placement. *The British Journal of Social Work*, 52(3): 1662–82. This article will support an empathic reflection on students' experiences of placement.

Chapter 8 | **Practice Educator Professional Standards for social work**

Chapter aims

» To consider how the requirements of Practice Educator Professional Standards for social work (PEPS) Stage 1 and Stage 2 assessment (BASW, 2022) may be met.

» To consider how the practice educator may maintain, develop and apply their learning.

Critical **questions**

» How will you engage with the PEPS assessment process?

» What support do you need to develop your practice educator skills and knowledge?

» How do you enhance the practice education provision in your placement agency?

» How will you ensure that you prioritise your own development as well as the student's learning needs?

Introduction

This chapter relates to Domain D of the PEPS (BASW, 2022) '*developing knowledge and continuing performance as a practice educator*'.

The PEPS (BASW, 2022) practice educator training is subdivided into Stage 1 and Stage 2. Each stage requires the qualifying practice educator to support, supervise and assess one student, and can be completed as two separate stages or as a two-year process. The qualifying practice educator is expected to demonstrate capability within all of the PEPS domains and statement of values. Each stage requires the qualifying practice educator to be supported by a mentor, and to be direct observed by the mentor at least once in each stage, but three times in total across both stages.

Following qualification as a practice educator, there is a further requirement for the practice educator to maintain currency.

Impact **of the pandemic**

Practice education training varies from area to area and in-person training remains relevant and important. Nevertheless, many trainings have become wholly or partially online due to the impact of the pandemic. This is helpful as pre-recorded lectures enable the practice educator to revisit the training at any point they wish to, thus making it more accessible. However, the need for reflective discussion to develop practice education knowledge, skills and values remains important; confidence in online discussion forums developed during the pandemic is often used to supplement practice educator training.

For both Stages 1 and 2, the practice educator should liaise with the local training provider to identify how training and assessment is currently undertaken, as well as seeking support from the mentor.

The chapter will support the practice educator to prepare for their own assessment at Stage 1 and Stage 2, including critical reflection and preparation for and incorporating feedback from the direct observation of the practice educator's practice. Furthermore, this will be followed by discussion of how the practice educator can maintain their currency of practice and enhance and develop their practice within new and related roles.

Critical reflection

This section can helpfully be read with Chapter 2 on preparation, which directs the practice educator to be aware of their values and the impact of power on the student, and Chapter 4 on critical reflection, which outlines the role of reflective practice and critical reflection. The PEPS Domain D4 (BASW, 2022) requires the practice educator to '*demonstrate critical reflection on their own development*'. While this chapter concludes this book, critical reflection on practice education knowledge and skills should *not* be left until the end of the student's placement. Instead, critical reflection on the role should be a continuous activity.

> ## Professional **development prompt**
>
> Critically reflect on your practice education knowledge and skills by considering:
>
> » feedback from the student on your role as a practice educator;
>
> » feedback from the mentor and tutor on your role as a practice educator;
>
> » your strengths and areas for development as a practice educator;
>
> » what practice education and adult learning theories you prefer;
>
> » how your legitimate power impacts on your role as a practice educator.
>
> (Adapted from Brookfield, 2017)

As a social worker and as a practice educator you are expected to be critically reflective, and this professional development prompt asks you to consider these different lenses. It is imperative to remember that in order to be critically reflective, you must implement your understanding from each of these questions to your practice.

Mentor support

Qualifying practice educators undertaking Stage 1 and/or Stage 2 of the PEPS (BASW, 2022) should be supported by a mentor. The mentor should be a qualified practice educator with experience of supporting a range of social work students. Their role, similar to the practice educator's role with a student, is to provide the education, support, management and assessment functions (ESMA) (Doel, 2010) to enable the practice educator to develop practice education knowledge and skills.

The first point of contact between practice educator and mentor should be before the student starts the placement, in the form of a planning meeting, where the mentor input can be discussed and agreed. Thereafter, the mentor should attend placement meetings (PLA and interim, and action plan if required) and provide monthly contact with the practice educator. The contact can be in the form of informal supervision and remote communication, or even email updates if the qualifying practice educator is progressing well in Stage 2. The mentor should provide support and advice, drawing on their practice wisdom and experience where the practice educator is dealing with challenges in the placement provision. In addition, the mentor should undertake, or arrange for another qualified practice educator to undertake, the direct observations of the practice educator, as will be discussed below. The mentor has final responsibility for the summative assessment of the student's placement, but ordinarily does this collaboratively with the practice educator. While it is rare that the qualifying practice educator and mentor disagree on the summative assessment in relation to the student, where this occurs, the mentor has the final say.

Finally, the mentor is required to make a summative assessment of the practice educator and make a recommendation that the qualifying practice educator has met the expectations of Stage 1 or 2, as appropriate. This should be done collaboratively by seeking the feedback of the student and tutor. Where the mentor identifies an area for development in relation to the practice educator's practice, it should be fed back to the practice educator in a timely and evidence-based manner during the student's placement. Of note, if the mentor has identified that the practice educator has not addressed areas for development, despite having support to address it, at the end of the student's placement, the mentor can recommend that the practice educator does not qualify at the appropriate PEPS stage at this time. This should be accompanied by recommendations for enhancing practice, which can include a reflective piece, having a further student or retaking the taught element of the practice educator training.

Direct observation of the qualifying practice educator

At both Stage 1 and Stage 2 of the PEPS (BASW, 2022), the qualifying practice educator is expected to be observed in their practice of supervising the student. In addition, there should be a third direct observation of the qualifying practice educator, which can be undertaken during Stage 1 or 2, and can be a student-related activity. The observer of the qualifying practice educator's practice must be a qualified practice educator.

It is wise to plan with the mentor when the direct observation will be undertaken, and it is strongly advised not to leave it until the end of the student's placement to avoid cancellation impacting on the ability to complete the practice education qualification. The best time to schedule an observed supervision is around the interim stage of the placement, as the supervisory relationship is developed and all the ESMA functions of social work student supervision (Doel, 2010) are fully operational. Although the observed supervision should be typical of supervision with the student, it can be helpful to ensure that it is more than case management discussion and could include, for example, feedback on the student's own direct observation, discussion about a specific theory, an activity planned to address an area for development or preparation for the interim meeting. Finally, ensure that any preparation for the supervision, such as pre-supervision reading or activity, is also distributed to the observer.

As with observation of the student's practice, it is helpful to undertake preparation and consideration of areas to be observed within the PEPS (BASW, 2022) domains and values. This will provide a focus for the observer and direct feedback accordingly. The direct observation of the supervision causes many qualifying practice educators some initial anxiety.

Professional **development prompt**

- » As you are preparing for your direct observation, reflect on how you feel.
- » Now consider how the student whom you will direct observe three times in their placement might be feeling as they prepare for a direct observation.
- » Can you identify ways that a student's potential fears and worries might be addressed?

It is helpful to reiterate that the purpose of the direct observation is an opportunity for the practice educator to gain developmental feedback about their professional practice. Indeed, it is an excellent opportunity to discuss and reflect upon your practice education knowledge and skills with the observer. However, it would not represent a reason to fail the practice educator training. Furthermore, using this insight into how it feels to be observed can be used as a learning opportunity to develop empathic understanding for the student's anxiety prior to their direct observations and to reflect on whether you can enhance your support to them.

Practice education training assessment processes may vary but most will require completion of a direct observation report or pro forma by the mentor and may require the qualifying practice educator to complete their own section. It is essential that the observer is afforded an opportunity to talk to the student after the direct observation to gather their feedback on the practice educator, and this should be recorded on the direct observation form. It is helpful to ensure that the mentor is able to provide verbal and written feedback soon after the direct observation. Finally, the direct observation form is usually required as part of the appropriate PEPS stage assessment process.

It is apt here to remind the qualifying practice educator that receiving feedback can be challenging, particularly when it does not align with our own perception of self (Carless and Boud, 2018). It is important to take time to reflect on the feedback; do not be afraid to ask to revisit it to enable further collaborative reflective discussion to support understanding of and engagement with the feedback.

Impact **of the pandemic**

The practice educator should arrange the direct observation to reflect the norm of supervision, so that if it is normally done through remote communication, the direct observation should also be done through remote communication. Or if the supervision is normally in person, then it should be observed in person.

Stage 1

To complete Stage 1 of the PEPS (BASW, 2022), practice educators are required to provide evidence of their achievements against learning outcomes in Domains A–D and the statement of values. It is important that the practice educator familiarises themself with the domains as they begin the practice educator training. They should revisit them through the student's placement to ensure that they are undertaking sufficient practice educating to enable them to confidently state that they have had the opportunity to demonstrate each and every domain.

As stated above, the assessment of Stage 1 varies between practice educator training providers, and the practice educator should familiarise themself with the requirements of their training. However, where there is an evidence folder requirement, it is advised that the practice educator regularly reviews the domains and allocates evidence to each domain, as leaving this until after the placement ends may leave them unable to meet certain criteria. In contrast, where the assessment criteria involve a written assessment, be that an academic piece or a reflection, it is often more helpful to complete this nearer the end of the student's placement or immediately after it ends, where learning from the practice educator role is both maximised and fresh.

Qualification at Stage 1 enables the practice educator to independently support and assess a first-placement student or support a final-placement student with the support of a mentor.

Stage 2

In order to complete Stage 2 of the PEPS (BASW, 2022), practice educators are required to provide evidence of meeting Domains A–D and the statement of values; a development of their practice education knowledge and skills; and be able to work increasingly autonomously in their role as practice educator.

Again, it is wise to check the practice educator training assessment, but it can include an evidence folder, academic work or reflection, and the advice above remains relevant. However, there may be an additional assessment at Stage 2, such as an oral examination. In this case, the qualifying practice educator will be asked questions to enable exploration of and reflection on their development aligned to the PEPS domains and statement of values. Provisional to the reflective engagement in the practice educator training process, this should be achievable for any practice educator who has supported a minimum of two social work students on placement. However, it should be noted that like any course, the qualifying practice educator will not automatically pass the practice educator training and may be asked to resubmit assessment work at Stage 1 or Stage 2 with further reflection on their practice.

Qualification at Stage 2 enables the practice educator to independently support and assess a first- or final-placement student.

Maintaining currency

Following Stage 2 qualification, the practice educator should continue to support social work students on placement within the practice educator role. Furthermore, moving into new areas of practice such as off-site practice educator (OSPE), practice educator mentor or practice education trainer can provide exciting opportunities for practice educators to develop their learning and expertise further. The practice educator can also engage with further developmental work with students and other learners, such as Assessed and Supported Year in Employment (ASYE) assessors, mentors and supervisors, recognising that the skills and knowledge of practice educators are relevant and can be applied to other contexts and those who are learning in a post-qualifying professional context.

However, it is important to note that to maintain the status of qualified practice educator, currency must be maintained. This requires the practice educator to have a student at least every two years, although they can have been involved in *other practice education activities*' (BASW, 2022, p 14), which can include co-facilitating practice educator training, mentoring practice educators in training, or undertaking practice education training.

Conclusion

This book is underpinned by the belief that practice educators need to engage in rigorous reflection, self-evaluation and openness to examination of their practice. It is only through the development of practice education knowledge and skills that the qualifying practice educator can provide a high-quality placement for the student, enabling them in turn to develop their social work knowledge and skills.

It is recognised that these are busy and challenging times for all practitioners and, for those who are also practice educators, their roles are usually taken in addition to their day jobs. However, it is essential that practice educators strive to maintain a focus on their own development as this will not only be of benefit to themselves but will also contribute to the development of the next generation of social workers and thus the service users whom the service provision supports.

We wish you luck and joy in your role as a practice educator, as it has always been our experience that the development of a student is a worthwhile and fulfilling activity.

Appendix 1: Sample supervision agreement

Student social worker: _____

Practice educator: _____

We will meet on a weekly basis for formal supervision. This will be for a period of an hour to 90 minutes.

Supervision will start promptly and cancellations kept to a minimum. If either party has to cancel, a satisfactory explanation should be given and the session rearranged as soon as possible. Interruptions to supervision will only be accepted in situations which require an immediate response.

Supervision should be a process based on an open and honest interaction between both parties. Both parties should attend organised and having reflected on the student's experiential learning opportunities. An agenda will be agreed at the start of each session.

Power issues will be openly acknowledged and addressed by both parties. All discussions will be carried out in an anti-discriminatory and anti-oppressive manner. Following discussion, if agreement or compromise cannot be reached on a given matter, advice and guidance will be sought from an appropriate third party, ie practice educator mentor, tutor, practice learning co-ordinator.

Standard agenda items are:

- » student well-being;
- » work undertaken by the student;
- » feedback on the student's development and areas for development;
- » application of theory to practice;
- » values and ethical dilemmas;
- » diversity and anti-oppressive practice;
- » student assessment, ie PCF domains;
- » training opportunities;
- » tasks to be completed;
- » other, please specify.

Discussions in supervision will contribute to assessment and will provide evidence for the final report/portfolio.

These meetings will be formally minuted electronically, and we will take turns to complete them. They will be checked/signed by both parties and copies kept. NB: Supervision records may need to be provided in the case of any dispute to provide evidence of actions agreed and taken.

Signed   _____   (Student)

          _____   (Practice educator)

          _____   (Date)

Appendix 2: Honey and Mumford's learning styles

(adapted from Honey and Mumford, 1992)

Type	Best learn and motivated by	Particularly like	Learn least from	Particularly dislike
Activists	• new experiences, problems or opportunities; • short spontaneous exercises, tasks and games; • excitement, drama, crisis and a variety of diverse activities; • being in the 'limelight', including chairing, leading and presenting; • being allowed to generate ideas without the constraints of practicality, policy or resource implications; • being involved in a difficult task; • being involved with others; • having a go (trying something for the first time).	• participating in new or novel experiences; • tackling real problems; • activities relating to future roles.	• taking a passive role, being asked to stand back and not get involved; • assimilating and analysing data; • working on their own; • being asked, before the learning event, to identify what they will learn and after the event, to appraise what they have learned; • being too theoretical; • being involved in repetitive activities; • being asked to carry out instructions with little room for manoeuvre; • being meticulous to detail.	• formulating objectives; • clarifying; • regularity; • imposed structure; • direct teaching inputs where they are expected to be passive or to sit on the sidelines.

Type	Best learn and motivated by	Particularly like	Learn least from	Particularly dislike
Reflectors	• being able to stand back, listen to and observe what is going on; • thinking before acting, having time to prepare; • carrying out research where they can investigate and assemble ideas; • reviewing what has happened and what they have learned; • being asked to produce carefully considered analyses; • exchanging views with other people in a safe, structured environment; • reaching decisions in their own time, without pressure and tight deadlines.	• observing someone else; • the opportunity to plan before action; • the opportunity to analyse; • reviewing; • thinking things over; • giving and getting feedback; • receiving help from others.	• being forced into the limelight, to take a lead; • situations which require action without planning; • short notice of an event they have to organise; • being given insufficient data on which to base a conclusion; • being given exact instructions of how things should be done; • being pressurised by time limits or rushed from one activity to the next; • having to take shortcuts or do a superficial job.	• performing without preparation.

Type	Best learn and motivated by	Particularly like	Learn least from	Particularly dislike
Theorists	• being offered (part of) a system, model, concept or theory; • having time to explore associations and inter-relationships between ideas, events and situations; • having the opportunity to question the rationale or logic behind something; • being pushed intellectually; • structured situations with a clear purpose; • ideas and concepts that emphasise rationality and logic (even if they do not appear immediately relevant); • being asked to analyse before being asked to generalise; • attempting to understand complex situations.	• a carefully prepared session; • situations where participation is structured; • intellectual activities; • considering the theory behind something.	• doing something without a context or apparent purpose; • situations which emphasise emotions or feelings; • unstructured activities and open-ended problem solving; • being asked to decide something without consideration to policy, principle or concept; • exploring something only superficially; • subject matter which is not statistically validated, has unsound methodology, is insufficient in evidence to support arguments; • situations where they feel different from the other learners.	• activities which encourage ambiguity and uncertainty; • ad hoc sessions.

Type	Best learn and motivated by	Particularly like	Learn least from	Particularly dislike
Pragmatists	• an obvious link between the subject matter and a problem; • techniques for doing things with obvious practical advantages (eg how to save time, revise better); • an opportunity to try out and practise and get feedback from a person they consider to be a good practitioner themselves; • a model which they can emulate; • situations where they can see that what they are doing is applicable to their job situation; • immediate implementation of what they have learned; • Concentration on practical issues (eg actions, plans, recommendations, etc). • situations where the learning activity is not seen to be related to a recognisable, immediate, practical benefit; • teachers who seem distant from reality.		• situations where there is no practice or clear guidelines on how to do a task; • situations where they cannot implement what they are learning; • situations where there is no apparent reward for the learning activity.	• moving outside their present role; • an absence of any link to reality.

References

Adams, R (2008) *Social Work and Empowerment*. London: Macmillan.

Argyris, C and Schön, D (1974) *Theory in Practice: Increasing Professional Effectiveness*. London: Jossey-Bass.

Banks, S (2021) *Ethics and Values in Social Work*. London: Red Globe Press.

Beckett, C, Maynard, A and Jordan, P (2017) *Values and Ethics in Social Work*. London: Sage.

Beddoe, L (2017) Harmful Supervision: A Commentary. *The Clinical Supervisor*, 36(1): 88–101.

Beesley, P (2022) Covid-19 Pandemic: A Threat or an Opportunity to Fieldwork Education in England? In Baikady, R, Sajid, S, Nadesan, V and Rezaul Islam, M (eds) *The Routledge Handbook of Field Work Education in Social Work* (pp 541–51). New Delhi: Routledge.

Beesley, P (2022) *Diligence and Collaboration: Practice Educators' and Students' Themed Narratives on Social Work Student Supervision*. PhD thesis. Leeds Beckett University.

Beesley, P and Taplin, S (2023) Blended Social Work Placements: Challenges and Opportunities. *Journal of Practice Teaching and Learning*, 20(1).

Beesley, P, Watts, M and Harrison, M (2018) *Developing your Communication Skills in Social Work*. London: Sage.

Black, P (1993) Formative and Summative Assessment by Teachers. *Studies in Science Education*, 21(1): 49–97.

Brandon, J and Davies, M (1979) The Limits of Competence in Social Work: The Assessment of Marginal Students in Social Work Education. *British Journal of Social Work*, 9(3): 295–347.

British Association of Social Workers (BASW) (2014) *Whistleblowing Policy*. [online] Available at: www.basw.co.uk/resources/basw-whistleblowing-policy (accessed 12 May 2023).

British Association of Social Workers (BASW) (2018) *Professional Capabilities Framework*. [online] Available at: www.basw.co.uk/system/files/resources/pcf-strat-social-worker.pdf (accessed 2 April 2023).

British Association of Social Workers (BASW) (2021) *The Code of Ethics for Social Work*. [online] Available at: www.basw.co.uk/about-basw/code-ethics (accessed 2 April 2023).

British Association of Social Workers (BASW) (2022) *Practice Educator Professional Standards (PEPS) for Social Work*. [online] Available at: www.basw.co.uk/social-work-training/practice-educator-professional-standards-peps (accessed 2 April 2023).

Brockbank, A and McGill, I (2007) *Facilitating Reflective Learning in Higher Education*. Maidenhead: McGraw-Hill Education.

Brodie, I and Williams, V (2013) Lifting the Lid: Perspectives on and Activity within Student Supervision. *Social Work Education*, 32(4): 506–22.

Brookfield, S (2017) *Becoming a Critically Reflective Teacher*. San Francisco: Jossey-Bass.

Brown, A and Bourne, I (1996) *The Social Work Supervisor*. Buckingham: Open University Press.

Burch, N (1970) Conscious Competence Learning Model: Four Stages of Learning Theory – Unconscious Incompetence to Unconscious Competence Matrix – and Other Theories and Models for Learning and Change. Attributed by Gordon Training to Noel Burch. [online] Available at: www.gordontraining.com (accessed 2 April 2023).

Burnham, J (2012) Developments in Social GGRRAAACCEEESSS: Visible-Invisible and Voiced-Unvoiced. In Krause, I (ed) *Culture and Reflexivity in Systemic Psychotherapy: Mutual Perspectives* (pp 139–60). London: Karnac.

Burt, M (2018) The 'Younghusband Report' Recommendation of Two-Year Training Courses and the Development of Social Work. *Practice: Social Work In Action*, 30(4): 223–6.

Caffrey, B and Fruin, H (2019) An Exploration of Issues Affecting the Assessment of Social Work Students on Practice Placement in England. *Journal of Practice Teaching and Learning*, 16(1–2): 68–82.

Calvin Thomas, G (2014) Meaningful Service User and Carer Involvement in Student Placements. In Fenge, L, Howe, K, Hughes, M and Calvin Thomas, G (eds) *The Social Work Portfolio: A Student's Guide to Evidencing Your Practice* (pp 69–82). Maidenhead: Open University Press.

Carless, D and Boud, D (2018) The Development of Student Feedback Literacy: Enabling Uptake of Feedback. *Assessment and Evaluation in Higher Education*, 43(8): 1315–25.

Caspi, J and Reid, W (2002) *Educational Supervision in Social Work: A Task-Centered Model for Field Instruction and Staff Development*. New York: Columbia University Press.

Central Council for Education and Training in Social Work (CCETSW) (1989) *Assuring Quality in the Diploma in Social Work (Paper 30)*. London: CCETSW.

Central Council for Education and Training in Social Work (CCETSW) (1991) *Rules and Requirements for the Diploma in Social Work: DipSW (Paper 30)*. London: CCETSW.

Cleak, H, Roulston, A and Vreugdenhill, A (2016) The Inside Story: A Survey of Social Work Students' Supervision and Learning Opportunities on Placement. *British Journal of Social Work*, 46(7): 2033–50.

Collingwood, P (2005) Integrating Theory and Practice: The Three-Stage Theory Framework. *Journal of Practice Teaching in Health and Social Work*, 6(1): 6–23.

Crenshaw, K (1989) Demarginalizing the Intersection of Race and Sex: A Black Feminist Critique of Anti-discrimination Doctrine, Feminist Theory and Anti-racist Politics. *University of Chicago Legal Forum*, 140: 139–67.

Croisdale-Appleby, D (2014) *Re-visioning Social Work Education: An Independent Review*. London: Department of Health.

Davys, A and Beddoe, L (2009) The Reflective Learning Model: Supervision of Social Work Students. *Social Work Education*, 28(8): 919–33.

Department for Education (DfE) (2018) *Post-qualifying Standard: Knowledge and Skills Statement for Child and Family Practitioners*. [online] Available at: https://assets.publishing.service.gov.uk/government/uploads/system/uploads/attachment_data/file/708704/Post-qualifying_standard-KSS_for_child_and_family_practitioners.pdf (accessed 2 April 2023).

Department of Health (DoH) (2002) *Requirements for Social Work Training*. [online] Available at: www.scie.org.uk/publications/guides/guide04/files/requirements-for-social-work-training.pdf?res=true (accessed 11 May 2023).

Department of Health (DoH) (2015) *Knowledge and Skills Statement for Social Workers in Adult Services*. [online] Available at: https://assets.publishing.service.gov.uk/government/uploads/system/uploads/attachment_data/file/411957/KSS.pdf (accessed 2 April 2023).

Dix, H (2018) Supervision within Placement: Achieving Best Practice. In Taplin, S (ed) *Innovations in Practice Learning* (pp 29–44). St Albans: Critical Publishing.

Doel, M (2010) *Social Work Placements: A Traveller's Guide*. Abingdon: Routledge.

Doel, M (2016) *Rights and Wrongs in Social Work: Ethical and Practice Dilemmas*. London: Palgrave.

Doel, M and Shardlow, S (2018) *The New Social Work Practice: Exercises and Activities for Training and Developing Social Workers*. Abingdon: Routledge.

Doran, G (1981) There's a SMART Way to Write Management's Goals and Objectives. *Management Review*, 70(11): 35–6.

Driscoll, J (2007) *Practising Clinical Supervision: A Reflective Approach for Healthcare Professionals.* Edinburgh: Elsevier.

Egan, R, Maidment, J and Connolly, M (2017) Trust, Power and Safety in the Social Work Supervisory Relationship: Results from Australian Research. *Journal of Social Work Practice*, 31(3): 307–21.

Fairtlough, A, Bernard, C, Fletcher, J and Ahmet, A (2014) Black Social Work Students' Experiences of Practice Learning: Understanding Differential Progression Rates. *Journal of Social Work*, 14(6): 605–24.

Ferguson, H (2018) How Social Workers Reflect in Action and When and Why They Don't: The Possibilities and Limits to Reflective Practice in Social Work. *Social Work Education*, 37(4): 415–27.

Finch, J (2017) *Supporting Struggling Students on Placement.* Bristol: Policy Press.

Finch, J and Taylor, I (2013) Failure to Fail? Practice Educators' Emotional Experiences of Assessing Failing Social Work Students. *Social Work Education: The International Journal*, 32(2): 244–58.

Fleming, N (2001) VARK: A Guide to Learning Styles. [online] Available at: www.vark-learn.com (accessed 2 April 2023).

Fook, J (2015) Reflective Practice and Critical Reflection. In Lishman, J (ed) *Handbook for Practice Learning in Social Work and Social Care: Knowledge and Theory* (pp 450–4). London: Jessica Kingsley.

Fook, J (2016) *Social Work: A Critical Approach to Practice.* London: Sage.

French, J and Raven, B (1959) The Bases of Social Power. In Cartwright, D (ed) *Studies in Social Power* (pp 311–20). Ann Arbor, MI: Institute for Social Research.

Furness, S (2012) Gender at Work: Characteristics of 'Failing' Social Work Students. *British Journal of Social Work*, 42(3): 480–99.

Furness, S and Gilligan, P (2004) Fit for Purpose: Issues from Practice Placements, Practice Teaching and the Assessment of Students' Practice. *Social Work Education*, 23(4): 465–79.

Gardiner, D (1988) *Teaching and Learning in Social Work Practice Placements: A Study of Process in Professional Education and Training.* University of London: EThOS.

Gardiner, F (2014) *Being Critically Reflective.* Basingstoke: Palgrave Macmillan.

General Social Care Council (GSCC) (2005) *Post Qualifying Education Framework for Social Work Education and Training.* London: General Social Care Council.

Gibbs, G (1988) *Learning by Doing: A Guide to Teaching and Learning Methods.* Oxford: Further Education Unit, Oxford Polytechnic.

Grant, L and Kinman, G (2013) *The Importance of Emotional Resilience for Staff and Students in the 'Helping Professions': Developing an Emotional Curriculum.* London: Higher Education Academy.

Green, P and Crisp, B (2007) Critical Incident Analyses: A Practice Learning Tool for Students and Practitioners. *Practice: Social Work in Action*, 19(1): 47–60.

Hair, H (2014) Power Relations in Supervision: Preferred Practices According to Social Workers. *Families in Society: The Journal of Contemporary Social Services*, 95(2): 107–14.

Hawkins, P and Shohet, R (1989) *Supervision in the Helping Professions.* Maidenhead: Open University Press.

Haynes, L (2019) *Social Work Sector Must Embrace Technology or Risk Being 'Left Behind', Says BASW Chief.* [online] Available at: www.communitycare.co.uk/2019/06/06/social-work-sector-must-embrace-technology-risk-left-behind-says-basw-chief/ (accessed 11 May 2023).

Hewson, M and Gant, V (2020) 'It's More Than Confusing our B's and D's': A Commentary on the Lack of Understanding of the Needs of Social Work Students Who Have Dyslexia. *Critical and Radical Social Work*, 8(2): 273–81.

Higgins, M (2019) Getting Started. In Mantell, A and Scragg, T (eds) *Reflective Practice in Social Work* (pp 19–38). London: Sage.

Hill, D, Agu, L and Mercer, D (2018) *Exploring and Locating Social Work: A Foundation for Practice*. London: Red Globe Press.

Hill, D and Frost, N (2018) Social Work in England: Regulation, Competition and Change. In Nieto-Morales, C (ed) *Social Work in the XXIst Century: Challenges to Educational and Professional Training* (pp 248–62). Madrid: Dykinson.

Hollinrake, S (2018) Anti-oppressive Practice, Social Work Values and Ethics. In Taplin, S (ed) *Innovations in Practice Learning* (pp 77–100). St Albans: Critical Publishing.

Honey, P and Mumford, A (1992) *The Manual of Learning Styles*. Maidenhead: Peter Honey Publications.

Hunt, R and Mathews, I (2018) Supporting Students with Dyslexia on Placement: Theory into Practice. In Taplin, S (ed) *Innovations in Practice Learning* (pp 121–36). St Albans: Critical Publishing.

Ingram, R (2013) Emotions, Social Work Practice and Supervision: An Uneasy Alliance? *Journal of Social Work Practice*, 27(1): 5–19.

Ingram, R (2015) *Understanding Emotions in Social Work: Theory, Practice and Reflection*. Maidenhead: Open University Press.

Institute for Apprenticeships and Technical Education (IATE) (2018) Social Worker (Integrated Degree). [online] Available at: www.instituteforapprenticeships.org/apprenticeship-standards/social-worker-integrated-degree-v1-0 (accessed 2 April 2023).

Irvine, J, Molyneux, J and Gillman, M (2015) 'Providing a Link with the Real World': Learning from the Student. Experience of Service User and Carer Involvement in Social Work Education. *Social Work Education*, 4(2): 138–50.

Jarvis, P and Gibson, S (1997) *The Teacher, Practitioner and Mentor in Nursing, Midwifery, Health Visiting and the Social Services*. Cheltenham: Nelson Thornes.

Jasper, M (2003) *Beginning Reflective Practice*. Cheltenham: Nelson Thornes.

Jasper, C and Field, P (2016) 'An Active Conversation Each Week in Supervision': Practice Educator Experiences of the Professional Capabilities Framework and Holistic Assessment. *British Journal of Social Work*, 46(6): 1636–53.

Kadushin, A (1976) *Supervision in Social Work*. New York, NY: Columbia University Press.

Kadushin, A and Harkness, D (2014) *Supervision in Social Work. Fifth Edition*. New York, NY: Columbia University Press.

Kanno, H and Koeske, G (2010) MSW Students' Satisfaction with their Field Placements: The Role of Preparedness and Supervision Quality. *Journal of Social Work Education*, 46(1): 23–38.

Ketner, M, Cooper-Bolinskey, D and VanCleave, D (2017) The Meaning and Value of Supervision in Social Work Field Education. *Field Educator*, 7(2): 1–18.

King-Owen, J (2020) *Service User Involvement in Social Work Education: A Case Study*. Citizen Network. [online] Available at: www.citizen-network.org/uploads/attachment/744/service-user-involvement-in-social-work-education.pdf (accessed 2 April 2023).

Knowles, M (1973) *The Adult Learner: A Neglected Species*. Houston, TX: Gulf Publishing.

Knowles, M, Holton III, E F, Swanson, R A and Robinson, P A (2020) *The Adult Learner: The Definitive Classic in Adult Education and Human Resource Development*. Abingdon: Routledge.

Kolb, D A (1984) *Experiential Learning: Experience as the Source of Learning and Development* (vol 1). Englewood Cliffs, NJ: Prentice-Hall.

Kotera, Y, Green, P and Sheffield, D (2018) Mental Health Attitudes, Self-criticism, Compassion and Role Identity Among UK Social Work Students. *British Journal of Social Work*, 49(2): 351–70.

Laming, W (2003) *The Victoria Climbié Inquiry*. [online] Available at: https://assets.publishing.service. gov.uk/government/uploads/system/uploads/attachment_data/file/273183/5730.pdf (accessed 11 May 2023).

Laming, W (2009) *The Protection of Children in England: A Progress Report*. [online] Available at: https:// assets.publishing.service.gov.uk/government/uploads/system/uploads/attachment_data/file/328117/ The_Protection_of_Children_in_England.pdf (accessed 11 May 2023).

Lave, J and Wenger, E (1991) *Situated Learning: Legitimate Peripheral Participation*. Cambridge: Cambridge University Press.

Lawler, J (2015) Motivation and Meaning: The Role of Supervision. *Practice – Social Work in Action*, 27(4): 265–75.

Lefevre, M (2005) Facilitating Practice Learning and Assessment: The Influence of Relationship. *Social Work Education*, 24(5): 565–83.

Leonard, K and O'Connor, L (2018) Transitioning from 'Outside Observer' to 'Inside Player' in Social Work: Practitioner and Student Perspectives on Developing Expertise in Decision-making. *Journal of Social Work Practice*, 32(2): 205–18.

Leung, K (2012) An Exploration of the Use of Power in Social Work Supervisory Relationships in Hong Kong. *Journal of Social Work Practice*, 26(2): 151–62.

Litvack, A, Bogo, M and Mishna, F (2010) Emotional Reactions of Students in Field Education: An Exploratory Study. *Journal of Social Work Education*, 46(2): 227–43.

Maclean, S, Finch, J and Tedam, P (2018) *SHARE: A New Model for Social Work*. Lichfield: Kirwin Maclean.

Maclean, S and Harrison, R (2014) *Social Work Theory: A Straightforward Guide for Practice Educators and Placement Supervisors*. Rugeley: Kirwin Maclean.

Mantell, A and Scragg, T (eds) (2019) *Reflective Practice in Social Work*. London: Sage.

Marton, F and Saljo, R (1976) On Qualitative Differences in Learning: 1. Outcome and Process. *British Journal of Educational Psychology*, 46(1): 4–11.

McCaughan, S, Hesk, G and Stanley, A (2018) Listening to Black Students: A Critical Review of Practice Education. In Taplin, S (ed) *Innovations in Practice Learning* (pp 101–20). St Albans: Critical Publishing.

Miehls, D, Everett, J, Segal, C and du Bois, C (2013) MSW Students' Views of Supervision: Factors Contributing to Satisfactory Field Experiences. *The Clinical Supervisor*, 32(1): 128–46.

Mishna, F, Milne, E, Bogo, M and Pereira, L F (2021) Responding to COVID-19: New Trends in Social Workers' Use of Information and Communication Technology. *Clinical Social Work Journal*, 49(4): 484–94.

Morris, B, Todd, S and Kalmanovitch, A (2022) When the Going Gets Tough: Case Studies of Challenge and Innovation in Canadian Field Education. In Baikady, R, Sajid, S, Nadesan, V and Rezaul Islam, M (eds) *The Routledge Handbook of Field Work Education in Social Work* (pp 156–71). New Delhi: Routledge.

Morrison, T (2005) *Staff Supervision in Social Care*. Brighton: Pavilion.

Mullin, W and Canning, J (2007) Process Recording in Supervision of Students Learning to Practice with Children. *Journal of Teaching in Social Work*, 27(3–4): 167–83.

Munro, E (2011) *The Munro Review of Child Protection: Final Report. A Child-Centred System*. London: Department for Education, HMSO.

Narey, M (2014) *Making the Education of Social Workers Consistently Effective.* [online] Available at: https://assets.publishing.service.gov.uk/government/uploads/system/uploads/attachment_data/file/287756/Making_the_education_of_social_workers_consistently_effective.pdf (accessed 2 April 2023).

O'Sullivan, T (2011) *Decision Making in Social Work.* London: Red Globe Press.

Office for Students (OfS) (2021) *Equality, Diversity and Student Characteristics Data: Students at English Higher Education Providers between 2010–11 and 2019–20.* [online] Available at: www.officeforstudents.org.uk/media/705bd553-189d-45a6-88a6-a16c9f3d96b8/equality-diversity-and-student-characteristics-data-june_2021.pdf (accessed 2 April 2023).

Ohno, T (1950s) Ask 'Why' Five Times About Every Matter. Toyota Myanmar. [online] Available at: www.toyota-myanmar.com/about-toyota/toyota-traditions/quality/ask-why-five-times-about-every-matter (accessed 2 April 2023).

Oliver, M (1990) *The Politics of Disablement.* London: Macmillan.

Rankine, M, Beddoe, L, O'Brien, M and Fouché, C (2018) What's Your Agenda? Reflective Supervision in Community-based Child Welfare Services. *European Journal of Social Work,* 21(3): 428–40.

Rogers, C (1967) *On Becoming a Person: A Therapist's View of Psychotherapy.* London: Constable.

Rolfe, G, Jasper, M and Freshwater, D (2011) *Critical Reflection in Practice.* London: Palgrave Macmillan.

Roulston, A, Cleak, H, Nelson, R and Hayes, D (2022) How Power Dynamics and Relationships Interact with Assessment of Competence: Exploring the Experiences of Student Social Workers Who Failed a Practice Placement. *The British Journal of Social Work,* 52(3): 1662–82.

Roulston, A, Cleak, H and Vreugdenhil, A (2018) Promoting Readiness to Practice: Which Learning Activities Promote Competence and Professional Identity for Student Social Workers During Practice Learning? *Journal of Social Work Education,* 54(2): 364–78.

Schön, D (1983) *The Reflective Practitioner.* London: Temple Smith.

Scragg, T (2019) Reflective Practice on Placement. In Mantell, A and Scragg, T (eds) *Reflective Practice in Social Work* (pp 139–54). London: Sage.

Shaia, W (2019) SHARP: A Framework for Addressing the Contexts of Poverty and Oppression During Service Provision in the United States. *Journal of Social Work Values and Ethics,* 16(1): 16–26.

Shardlow, S and Doel, M (1993) Examination by Triangulation: A Model for Practice Teaching. *Social Work Education,* 12(3): 67–79.

Shulman, L (1993) *Interactional Supervision.* Washington, DC: NASW Press.

Sicora, A (2019) Reflective Practice and Learning from Mistakes in Social Work Student Placement. *Social Work Education,* 38(1): 63–74.

Simmonds, J (2018) Relating and Relationships in Supervision: Supportive and Companionable or Dominant and Submissive? In Ruch, G, Turney, D and Ward, A (eds) *Relationship-based Social Work: Getting to the Heart of Practice* (pp 221–35). London: Jessica Kingsley.

Smale, G, Tuson, G and Biehal, N (1993) *Empowerment, Assessment, Care Management and the Skilled Worker.* London: HMSO.

Social Care Institute for Excellence (SCIE) (2017) *Effective Supervision in a Variety of Settings.* [online] Available at: www.scie.org.uk/publications/guides/guide50 (accessed 2 April 2023).

Social Work England (SWE) (2019) *Qualifying Education and Training Standards 2019.* [online] Available at: www.socialworkengland.org.uk/media/1641/socialworkengland_ed-training-standards-2019_final.pdf (accessed 2 April 2023).

Social Work England (SWE) (2020) *Professional Standards.* [online] Available at: www.socialworkengland.org.uk/standards/professional-standards (accessed 2 April 2023).

Social Work England (SWE) (2021) A Guide to Fitness to Practise. [online] Available at: www.socialwork england. org.uk/concerns/fitness-to-practise-guide (accessed 2 April 2023).

Stone, C (2018) Transparency of Assessment in Practice Education: The TAPE Model. *Social Work Education*, 37(8): 977–94.

Taplin, S (ed) (2018) *Innovations in Practice Learning*. St Albans: Critical Publishing.

Tedam, P (2012) The MANDELA Model of Practice Learning: An Old Present in New Wrapping? *Journal of Practice Teaching and Learning*, 11(3): 60–76.

Tedam, P (2014) When Failing Doesn't Matter: A Narrative Inquiry into the Social Work Practice Learning Experiences of Black African Students in England. *International Journal of Higher Education*, 3(1): 136–45.

Tedam, P (2021) *Anti-oppressive Social Work Practice*. London: Sage.

The College of Social Work (TCSW) (nd) *Principles for Gathering and Using Feedback from People Who Use Services and Those Who Care for Them*. [online] Available at: https://coercivecontrol.ripfa.org.uk/wp-content/uploads/TCSW_Assessing_social_work_practice_against_the_PCF-principles_for_gathering_feedback.pdf (accessed 2 April 2023).

Thompson, N (1997) *Anti-Discriminatory Practice*. London: Palgrave Macmillan.

Thompson, N (2021) *Anti-Discriminatory Practice: Equality, Diversity and Social Justice*. London: Red Globe Press.

Thompson, N and Pascal, J (2011) Reflective Practice: An Existentialist Perspective. *Reflective Practice: International and Multidisciplinary Perspectives*, 12(1): 15–26.

Tsui, M (2005) *Social Work Supervision: Contexts and Concepts*. London: Sage.

Turner, D (ed) (2021) *Social Work and Covid-19*. St Albans: Critical Publishing.

Tversky, A and Kahneman, D (1974) Judgment under Uncertainty: Heuristics and Biases. *Science*, 185(4157): 1124–31.

VARK: A Guide to Learning Styles. [online] Available at: www.vark-learn.com (accessed 2 April 2023).

Vygotsky, L (1978) *Mind and Society: The Development of Higher Psychological Processes*. Cambridge, MA: Harvard University Press.

Wachtel, T and McCold, P (2001) Restorative Justice in Everyday Life. In Braithwaite, J and Strang, H (eds) *Restorative Justice and Civil Society* (pp 114–28). Cambridge: Cambridge University Press.

Wallcraft, J, Fleischmann, P and Schofield, P (2012) *The Involvement of Users and Carers in Social Work Education: A Practice Benchmarking Study*. London: SCIE.

Whittington, C (2003) Collaboration and Partnership in Context. In Weinstein, J, Whittington, C and Leiba, T (eds) *Collaboration in Social Work Practice* (pp 13–38). London: Jessica Kingsley.

Williams, S and Rutter, L (2021) *The Practice Educator's Handbook*. London: Learning Matters.

Wilson, E and Flanagan, N (2021) What Tools Facilitate Learning on Placement? Findings of a Social Work Student-to-Student Research Study. *Social Work Education*, 40(4): 535–51.

Wonnacott, J (2012) *Mastering Social Work Supervision*. London: Jessica Kingsley.

Yeung, E, Newman, A and Burke, B (2021) Navigating Relationships in Practice Learning: Voices from Practice Educators. *Social Work Education,* 40(3): 412–24.

Young, P and Burgess, H (2004) Dancing on a Moving Carpet: The Changing Context. In Burgess, H and Taylor, I (eds) *Effective Learning and Teaching in Social Policy and Social Work* (pp 21–5). Abingdon: Routledge.

Younghusband, E (1959) *Report of the Working Party on Social Workers in the Local Authority Health and Welfare Services*. London: HMSO.

Index

Note: Page numbers in *italics* denote figures.

For Product Safety Concerns and Information please contact our EU
representative GPSR@taylorandfrancis.com
Taylor & Francis Verlag GmbH, Kaufingerstraße 24, 80331 München, Germany

www.ingramcontent.com/pod-product-compliance
Lightning Source LLC
Chambersburg PA
CBHW050443280326
41932CB00013BA/2218